THE
SOCIAL CALENDAR

The
Social Calendar

ANNA SPROULE

BLANDFORD PRESS
Poole   ·   *Dorset*

By the same author
Port Out, Starboard Home

Produced by MIDAS BOOKS

First published in 1978 by
Blandford Press Ltd.
Link House, West Street,
Poole, Dorset BH15 1LL

©Anna Sproule 1978

ISBN 0 7137 8523 3

Printed in Great Britain by
Chapel River Press, Andover, Hampshire

Contents

Acknowledgments

The author and publishers would like to thank the Bodley Head for their kind permission to allow excerpts from *The Edwardians* by Vita Sackville-West to be reprinted here.

In addition, Anna Sproule would like to express her personal thanks to Lady Elizabeth Anson, of Party Planners, and to the Press Office of the Dorchester Hotel, for the invaluable insights they gave her into the modern social calendar; to the 'thirties deb' of Chapter 13 and all the other informants quoted, for their help, great patience, and trust that their anonymity would be preserved; and to Sara Sproule, for the hours spent finding and deciphering family correspondence of the last century.

The publishers wish to express their gratitude to the following picture libraries for the illustrations used in this book:

Mary Evans Picture Library—Society tea-party; London Zoo; The Victorian ball; 1877—meeting Her Majesty at Buckingham Palace; Hyde Park waiting for Princess Alexandra; Presentation queue; High fashions for the ladies; British residents in Pekin; Accessory to the fact—lady's maid; Parasols at Ascot; Eton and Harrow match; Henley by night; Riding in Rotten Row; Frontispiece, polo.

Popperfoto—Débutantes at Queen Charlotte's Ball; Dinner table of the 1930s; Fashion after the First World War; Fashion in the 1930s; Fashions in the holidays—the sun deck; Tea in Bangalore; The Ootacamund Hunt; Umbrellas at Ascot; Henley 1892 by day; Cowes 1930; Hunting in November; The last débutante 1958.

Hulton Library—Fashion in the Edwardian Period.

Press Association—Fashion in 1910; 1910's 'Black Ascot'.

Country Life—Royal Yachting late in Nineteenth Century; Heading towards freedom, bicycles; Croquet on the lawn.

Central Press Photos—Royal Garden Party 1976.

Fox Photos—Chelsea Arts Ball.

Foreword

A hundred years and twenty-seven months separate the accession of Queen Victoria in June 1837 and the outbreak of the Second World War in 1939. In the period bracketed by these two conveniently symbolic dates, the topmost section of British society—followed, with local variations, by that of most of the English-speaking world—brought a new degree of method to the time-honoured pursuit of turning play into something very like work. In so doing, it built up an institution of quite extraordinary complexity, practical usefulness, and strength: the social calendar of the nineteenth and early twentieth centuries.

In this book, I hope to give some idea as to just how complex, useful and strong that remarkable institution was, together with an indication of its still-abiding influence. Three caveats, however, should first be expressed.

The first concerns terminology. I have deliberately opted for the traditional class labels of 'upper', 'upper-middle' and 'middle' for the people I am writing about. Nothing else quite fitted. The concept of gentle birth, hard to define at the best of times, is now fast becoming obsolete; obsolete enough, at least, to make constant further definition necessary. By the same token, the apparently more straightforward notion of 'Society', with a capital letter, in fact requires considerable qualification and explanation. The modern socio-economic groupings—A, B, C1 and so on—are, of course, hopelessly inappropriate. So 'upper' and 'upper-middle' it has to be; if terms like these are not as precise as might be wished, they have the merit of being instantly, even intuitively, comprehensible.

My second warning concerns money. At no point have I tried to carry out the nigh-impossible task of giving up-to-date equivalents for the sums of money mentioned in the course of this book. A far more accurate idea of how, say, it felt to spend £50 on a dress in the middle-to-late Victorian period is gained by absorbing the internal evidence of the time: in particular, the incomes and wages levels referred to by contemporary writers. A useful example of one such 'incomes table'—an upper-class one—is found on page 104.

My third point may, perhaps, be an unnecessary one. Since my aim is to study the social calendar as a phenomenon in its own right, I have made little explicit reference to the activities and living conditions of those outside the charmed circle. A knowledge of the black side of British life is something that can now, I feel, be taken for granted, and I have therefore assumed throughout that readers will make all the necessary comparisons for themselves.

The Prince and Princess of Wales receiving guests at a Garden Party at Marlborough House (1878).

CHAPTER ONE

∞∞

A Social Calendar

It is a fine, decorous, expensive, Protestant carnival.
Henry James on the London Season,
the *Century Magazine,* 1888

In 1897, the year of Queen Victoria's Diamond Jubilee, the
Derby was won for the first time in its history by an Irish
horse: the favourite, Galtee More, owned by a Mr John
Gubbins. The Eton and Harrow match at Lord's resulted in a
draw for the fourth year running. A new theatre—Her
Majesty's—was opened in the Haymarket and introduced to
its first audience with a special poem from the Poet Laureate
and a rendering of the National Anthem by Miss Clara Butt;
'these interesting preliminaries', commented *The Times*
austerely, 'encroached rather seriously upon the time
allotted to the play.' A lady presented to the Sovereign
suffered the rare social disgrace of having the event
subsequently cancelled, since her qualifications had not
proved adequate on examination. The London Season was
dominated by the Jubilee celebrations themselves and by a
fancy dress ball given by the Duchess of Devonshire for a
thousand guests. The grouse were a failure, and fishing
everywhere was terrible: a sea serpent, however, was sighted
off Dundee. (True, no one tried to catch it, but only from
want of opportunity; the first hoopoe ever to have been seen
in Great Britain after early autumn was promptly gunned
down on 28 October.) The fat and charming Duchess of
Teck—mother of the Duchess of York, later Queen
Mary—died. The Duchess of Hamilton married a plain Mr
Forster. And exceptional storms and flooding hit the East
Coast, causing damage so extensive in places that, experts
reckoned, reclamation would cost more than the land was
worth.

There is a pattern behind this apparent hotchpotch of
occurrences. They are a selection from the social and
sporting events of the year, and, except for the first and last,

all of them had their main impact on the topmost section of British society: on the people who went to the theatre, read *The Times,* danced till dawn in Mayfair and waded thigh-high in provokingly empty rivers. Then as now, the Derby was democratic in its appeal, while the floods were all-encompassing in their effects; but the horse—and landowning classes certainly had a keen interest in both matters. And, while Mr Gubbins could not have been completely sure that the favourite he owned would win, and while no landowner could have reckoned on the total disappearance of some of his property, there was an extraordinary amount of 1897 that both—along with their wives, acquaintances and whole social class—could have plotted out in advance.

They knew, for example, that from the end of April to the latter part of July London would be crowded with the four thousand richest, smartest and/or noblest families in the land (by that period, being smart by no means meant being noble as well). They knew that, within this space of time, a welter of events would take place: the opening of the Covent Garden opera season; the Royal Drawing Rooms at Buckingham Palace; innumerable parties, private concerts, balls; the Eton and Harrow match; the Henley Regatta; the weekly 'church parade' in Hyde Park; polo at Ranelagh; lawn tennis at various places, one of which was Wimbledon; Royal Ascot; garden parties; and Goodwood, which traditionally closed the Season.

According to their means and inclinations, they were prepared to take part in as many of these fixtures as they could; and they also intended to follow them up with an August and September by the sea, or by some fabled salmon river, or at a foreign spa, or on a grouse moor. October saw the opening of the pheasant season; hunting started in November and continued until March or April, according to the pack with which the enthusiast hunted. Racing continued practically the year through and superimposed its own timetable on a social programme that already presented a highly complicated blend of culture, sport and plain entertainment.

To a far greater degree than their eighteenth-century forebears, the upper-class Victorians knew just what they would be doing with themselves at any given time of the year—in outline, at least. In the eighty or so years covering their Queen's reign and the period immediately preceding it, they had evolved for themselves not merely a social round but a whole social calendar: a calendar studded with fixed points of interest that reached from the year's beginning to the year's end. How the gaps between these points were filled in was up to the participants themselves; but, while the details depended largely on the wealth of those concerned, on their social prestige and—unsurprisingly—on the weather, the overall picture that emerged was a remarkably homogeneous one. The social calendar of the Top Victorians exercised a spell over both upper and upper-middle classes that was too strong ever to be entirely denied.

This is how, in that Jubilee Year, they obeyed some of its demands.

January

Race meetings are held at Newmarket, Gatwick, Windsor and elsewhere. Cause of conversation: will the new starting-machine, an object of interest and controversy, be introduced on Irish race-courses?

Hunting is patchy. At a meet in Newark Market Place, the Mayor entertains leading members of the hunt in the Corporation Buildings. The rain and the hounds turn up simultaneously at eleven o'clock; the hunt finally moves off through the downpour at a sharp trot. The star of the show earns a commendation from the magazine *Country Life,* then in its first month of existence: 'he must have been a good fox, to stand before hounds as he did for 48 minutes and then beat them.'

Pheasant-shooting closes at the end of the month; there are too many cock pheasant left, complains a *Country Life* correspondent. (The explanation is that his pheasant shoot last November took place in thrashing rain and his December one in a blizzard.) However, the bag after lunch during his last shoot of the season consists of forty-nine rabbits, a woodcock, two pigeons, three hares, one partridge—and only ten pheasants.

Mid-January ice is followed by blizzards; sport everywhere comes to a standstill. London traffic is in utter confusion, with omnibus and van horses falling victim by the score to ice-bound streets. The snow is followed by floods.

At a ballad concert at Queen's Hall, London, Mr Plunket Green's rendering of 'Star of Eve' from *Tannhäuser* is much admired by those who brought themselves to venture out.

February

At Sandown Park, the Sandown Grand Prize is won by Knight of Rhodes. Cause of conversation: chances for the Grand National and the Lincoln.

The first post-floods meet of the Quorn takes place. Those present include the Duke of Marlborough, Viscountess Curzon, Sir Henry and Lady Meysey-Thompson, Lord Henry Paulet, Captain the Hon. Henry Molyneux, the Baron and Baroness Max de Tuyll and others.

The Waterloo Cup, the premier event of the hare-coursing year, is won by a third-season fawn dog called Gallant, bought by its owner for £50 and reckoned cheap at the price.

To raise funds to build the London Homeopathic Hospital, the Prince of Wales holds a skating fête; spectators include the Duchess of Devonshire (soon to distinguish herself by giving the most glittering ball of the year) and the Duchess of Teck (soon to die).

March

Manifesto wins the Grand National; Winkfield's Pride the Lincoln Handicap.

The Duke of York—the future George V—opens a sale and exhibition of Irish industries at Chelsea House. The Countess of Becktive and her daughter—who, gushed a commentator, looked like sisters—sold cushions 'over which everyone went into raptures'.

April

London starts to fill up: the authorities at Hyde Park, predicting big business in the Jubilee Year, stock up with several hundred new green chairs for promenaders to sit on. A M. Lucien Hardy announces in *The Times* that he has arrived in town for the Season and solicits queries on concert engagements. Similarly, a Madame Stainton Taylor 'will receive ladies together or privately to prepare for presentation to Her Majesty the Queen'.

A private view at the New Gallery is slightly under-attended; absentees may have had feelings similar to those of non-exhibitor Stanhope Forbes, who tells reporters that he has reserved his works for the 'big show' at the Royal Academy. Those present, however, have a chance to savour the appalling silence that falls when one visitor knocks over a valuable statuette. It was, says the *Lady* in its account of the event, 'irreparably injured'.

May

The London Season officially opens: its traditional starting-signal is the Private View at the Royal Academy, held in the first week of the month. Those attending include Prince Edward of Saxe-Weimar, the Duchess of Cleveland, the Japanese Minister and his wife, and an exquisite woman in grey who is escorted by Anthony Hope of *Zenda* fame. Mysteriously, Mr Hope refuses to reveal her identity. One visitor, more outspoken than the rest, says that she plans to look at the pictures during the morning only; the afternoon will be spent talking to her friends.

Church Parade—the after-church saunter in the Stanhope Gate area of Hyde Park—becomes more thickly attended each week. On Sunday evenings, before-dinner saunterers can hear a band of Life Guards. They can hear another Guards band in Green Park if they wish; but Green Park is not fashionable.

The garden party season starts, one of the first being that of the Wheel Club, held at Hereford House. The craze for bicycling is now at its height; but the lady club-members, though they bring their machines to the party, find the weather too hot for exercise.

Two Court Drawing Rooms take place. Nearly three hundred girls and women are presented, either to Queen Victoria or to the Princess of Wales (the Queen, clinging firmly to her habit of seclusion, only stays for an hour). It is noticed that the débutantes' bouquets are this year being constructed on the 'shower' principle rather than the nosegay one: a shower bouquet, an expert explains, is easier to hold gracefully, contains fewer flowers, and is cheaper.

The curtain goes up on the first night of Covent Garden's opera season; both the Prince and Princess of Wales are present, but in separate boxes. The Princess of Wales also attends the Royal Military Tournament, the show of the Royal Horticultural Society at the Inner Temple and a State Concert. Society observers admire her youthfulness; it seems absurd that she should have three grown-up daughters. (She will, in fact, keep one of these with her as companion and captive until her own death.)

Among theatre-goers, matinées are now the thing. Addicts can attend morning matinées, afternoon matinées, even evening matinées. An afternoon matinée offered at the Olympic is that safe stand-by, *Antony and Cleopatra*. The Globe, in contrast, is offering Ibsen's *Wild Duck*; Society, complains an Ibsen fan, does not seem to have taken to it.

A concert is held at Bridgewater House, residence of Lord and Lady Ellesmere, in aid of the North St Pancras Children's Holiday Fund; a Primrose League Rally takes place at the Royal Albert Hall. At a flower ball given by Mrs Oppenheim, guests who felt that they had done their job by loading themselves with fresh flowers soon wish they'd been more original: Mrs Asquith goes one better by dressing from head to heels as a 'red, red rose', while Lily, Duchess of Marlborough appears as—a lily.

The news seeps through that Lord and Lady Warwick intend to give a grand municipal garden party for five thousand at Warwick Castle: all burgesses and their wives invited. (When the party takes place, numbers have been pruned to a more manageable thousand.)

June

Galtee More wins the Derby.

The boys of Eton, with their fathers, mothers and sisters, celebrate The Fourth. There are speeches (most of them now in English rather than Latin), toasts, the cricket match, the procession of boats led by the ten-oared *Monarch*, and fireworks featuring a set piece showing the Eton College arms. Top parents this year are the Duke and Duchess of

Connaught, son and daughter-in-law of the Queen. Contrary to tradition, weather on the day stays fine.

Invitations to the Duchess of Devonshire's fancy ball—speculated on for weeks—finally go out; an end to speculation, perhaps, but the beginning of considerable heart-burning among the uninvited. An additional topic of conversation is the concert being organised by Mr Astor, 'the programme of which', the *Lady* comments, 'is such as only a millionaire's cheque-book or pure charity can attempt.' Paderewski and Mme Melba are among those who will perform: Melba's fees are the highest in the business, and Paderewski's run her close.

The fine weather holds for Ascot week: too fine, from the racing point of view, since the ground is iron-hard and covered with bare patches. The Prince and Princess of Wales lead the Royal Procession of six carriages down the course. The main fashion point is the feather boa. *The Times* notes the glittering presence in the Royal Enclosure of visiting Indian dignitaries, in England for the Jubilee celebrations; also the complaints made about the outlying presence of beggars, loafers, gypsies 'and other vagrants'. A brief moment of horror occurs when a man steps out onto the course during the first race, causing near-collision among the horses. The Gold Cup is won by the Prince of Wales's own horse, Persimmon, then at the height of his racing career; 'class', *Country Life* comments, 'will always beat handicap form'.

Ascot dresses get their second showing at a fête and gymkhana at the Ranelagh Club. The most popular event of the afternoon is the Victoria Cross race: each competitor dashes up on horseback to a 'wounded soldier', loads him on and returns to the finishing-post. The 'soldiers' are dummies: the horses, not caring for them one bit, increase the jollity by refusing to stand still and be loaded.

In London, hotels are bursting at the seams. Late-coming Jubilee visitors can count themselves lucky if they secure a servant's bedroom in the attic. The scaffolding for the stands lining the procession route to St Paul's goes up in a last-minute rush, and a timber famine hits the city. Every Society woman with a seat on the route goes shopping for new clothes; a particular favourite is a dress of pleated chiffon in red, white and blue. On 22 June, the Queen makes her six-mile Jubilee drive through London in dazzling sunshine; 'the crowds', she wrote afterwards, 'were quite indescribable, and their enthusiasm truly marvellous and deeply touching.'

A gala Jubilee performance is given at Covent Garden to an audience that included sixty royalties, while an 'At Home' held by Mrs Alan Gardner in honour of another of Victoria's sons, the Duke of Saxe-Coburg and Gotha, attracts the presence of several Indian princes, the Austrian, German, Japanese and Chinese Ambassadors, a selection of foreign and British aristocracy (including the ubiquitous Duchess of Cleveland) and the special Persian envoy, His Excellency the Nasir-ul-Mulk.

Lawn tennis starts to exert its spell. 'Wimbledon', says a *Lady* correspondent, 'is quite one of the nicest lawn tennis meetings. If you arrive in comfortable time for tea, you are pretty sure to find that the matches of the day are yet to come off, thus comfort and the very best tennis are happily combined in a way unknown to those harassed audiences and players who are elsewhere victimised at the hottest hours of the morning.' But a large part of Society moves temporarily out of London to Portsmouth, where the Jubilee Naval Review is being held.

A reception given by the American wife of millionaire and former Secretary for the Colonies, Joseph Chamberlain, leads to total discomfiture on the part of both hostess and guests. Too many invitations go out; the crowds prevent the Chamberlains' guest of honour, the Prince of Wales, from entering the house, and his youngest daughter is jostled on the pavement. The Prince is 'white with fury'.

July

The Duchess of Devonshire give her long-awaited fancy dress ball. Historical personages represented by the royalty, nobility and gentry who attend include: the Queen of Scots, Marie Antoinette, Zenobia (the hostess's own choice), Mme de Pompadour, Peg Woffington, the Queen of Sheba, Anne of Cleves, Charlotte Corday, Cleopatra and Guinevere. There is one Dawn, one Britannia and—upsettingly—more than one Brunhilde. At a gala day shortly afterwards at Hurlingham, spectators divide their time between the polo and dissection of the Devonshire event.

The Oxford v. Cambridge and Eton v. Harrow matches take place at Lord's in the same week. Those attending can be easily divided into those for whom the game is the thing, those to whom the game gives a chance to meet their old friends (easily the biggest group) and those for whom the game is a mere excuse for a picnic. The Eton and Harrow match is left drawn; Cambridge wins by 179 runs.

London begins to empty: there is a rush to get dinners, dances and balls in before it empties completely. Vacant chairs are noticed in the Park during Church Parade.

Henley—a fine-weather Henley—comes and goes; London empties still further.

The Opera season closes, and there are complaints that not a single British work has been performed. The favourites, this year and always, are invariably Wagner, Meyerbeer, Gounod and Verdi.

The Duke of Richmond's race-meeting at Goodwood is attended by the Waleses and the Dukes and Duchesses of York and Devonshire. The assembly is smart, the racing rather medium. The Goodwood Stakes is judged to be 'as miserable an affair as it is possible to conceive'; the Goodwood Cup is won by Count Schomberg.

August

London moves temporarily to Brighton, to Ostend, to the north-west coast of France (Dinard is an up-and-coming resort) and to Cowes. Light winds spoil much of the racing here; on shore, the ladies reject feather boas in favour of blue and white serge, topped by modified sailor hats. 'The really great event of the life here', comments one sceptic, 'is the number of people who will pay you a visit on purpose to tell you that the Prince has just called at their yacht, or that he was there last night. If he has been to see half the people who say he has, his social obligations must have taken up all his time.'

Owing to disease on the moors, grouse prospects look doubtful, although the record bag in Yorkshire on the Glorious Twelfth is three hundred brace. The doubts, though, are eventually fulfilled, and sportsmen's dreams start turning to 1 September and the partridge season.

Meanwhile, their children have their first training in handling a gun. 'Certainly', says *Country Life* cheerfully,

> we may send [a boy] out with a lighter heart now than in the old days of muzzle-loaders, when there was that complicated arrangement of caps and powder, flasks and shot belts, which is all included now in the small neat space of a cartridge. With all a boy's ingenuity in the way of getting himself into mischief, it is hard to see how he will injure himself in the process of loading. Very possibly he will blow some of his fingers off subsequently, but it is something to think that he can make his preparations in tolerable safety.

Country-house parties organise tennis tournaments, gymkhanas, picnics; coastal and river regattas carry on through the month.

In Devon, the stag-hunting season opens.

September

Partridges are not quite as plentiful as expected; the Yorkshire rivers, however, have improved.

The last cricket matches of the year are played, and lawn tennis closes its season with a tournament in Brighton.

In London, Regent's Street is half up, and traffic is diverted into Soho and Mayfair. An observer watching the departure of women's rational dress promoters to their conference in Oxford noted that each and every one of them wore a skirt for their journey. They did not change into their trousers until their conference banquet.

Galtee More scores another racing victory for John Gubbins by coming first in the St Leger.

In Scotland, a 'large and fashionable' ball is held at Aberfeldy, while those members of the upper classes remaining south of the border divide their time fitfully between the country and the grander London hotels. The Hon. Maurice Gifford and Miss Marguerite Thorold are married before a large congregation at St Paul's, Knightsbridge; the groom lost one of his arms at the defence of Bulawayo, and among the presents to his bride is a bracelet of Matabele gold inset with the bullet that the army doctor extracted from his shoulder.

Hunting prospects look good, and cubbing starts with the Bedale Hounds.

October

The Prince and Princess of Wales return to England from overseas: the Princess from her native Denmark, the Prince from Marienbad, where he has taken the cure in company with King Alexander of Serbia, the Princess of Montenegro, the Gladstones and others.

Pheasants are plentiful, although not many are shot so early in the season. Cubbing is good, especially in Ireland. Partridges, after a shaky start, are now reckoned a success.

The Scottish season for sport and social gatherings continues; so, in London, does the season for Society weddings. The Marquis of Waterford marries Lady Beatrix FitzMaurice at St George's, Hanover Square; less conventionally, a Sir Edwin Arnold marries a Japanese bride 'very quietly', at St Mathias', Earl's Court.

The Duchess of Teck dies; the hoopoe is shot.

November

The hunting season starts. The Bedale Hounds go out frequently; the Old Surrey at Coulsdon has one of the largest attendances at its opening meet for years. Foxes are plentiful, the weather stays open, and enthusiasts are delighted. After heavy rain strips coverts of foliage, shooting takes a new lease of life: a bag of seven hundred head is recorded in Yorkshire.

The County Ball season gets under way.

December

East Coast and Cinque Ports areas are ravaged by floods, although North Sussex suffers a drought. The High Sheriff of Suffolk holds a fancy dress ball.

A four-day partridge shoot at Holkham Hall, the Earl of Leicester's Norfolk estate, results in a total partridge bag of

2423. In addition, three pheasants, fifty-five hares and seven 'various' are shot, making an all-round total of 2488 head.

A second hoopoe is shot in Sussex, and it is hopefully pointed out that a third must be around somewhere, since hoopoes mate for life.

It is legally ruled that a man who tramped across a Yorkshire moor, opening and shutting an umbrella as he went, had in fact no right to do so. (His aim was to frighten the birds preserved by the moor's owner, against whom he had a grudge.) In future, he is told, he may only use the moor footpath, and 'even there to keep the demonstration of his umbrella within due limits'.

Frost sets in, and all but the skaters—who have been practising their techniques at London's Niagara Rink—make the best they can of their enforced holiday from sport by celebrating Christmas.

Presented at Court, 1881

CHAPTER TWO

⌒⌒⌒

The Rule Book

It is a good thing for everyone that there are rules by which Society, now that it has become so vast and complicated a machine, is held together and enabled to work smoothly and easily.

The *Lady*, February 1893

Spring and early summer in London, autumn and winter in the country: that is one of the main patterns emerging from the mass of events which, for Britain's leisured classes, gave 1897 its particular flavour. Another is the extraordinarily split-minded passion for things that ran, flew or swam: before its date with the beaters, a hand-reared pheasant received every bit as much loving care as Persimmon and Galtee More. A third is found in the frequency with which some of the names recur. The Duchess of Devonshire was at this, the Duchess of Cleveland went to that, the Prince of Wales and his wife were noticed severally or together at the Opera, at Ascot, at Cowes, on the pavement outside an over-crowded reception.

Otherwise, the events tend to blur: all that's left is an impression of diamonds, titles, parties, wet countryside, along with the feeling that hits one after reading the whole weddings page in a local newspaper at one sitting. The upper-class Victorians have confirmed our general idea that they did themselves prodigally proud and have indicated some of the methods that they brought to the business. What is less apparent from our portrait of a year is that the whole thing—the seasonal drift between town and country, the enthusiasm for field sports, the *de rigueur* element present in so many of the activities, the tightly-knit nature of the groups taking part—adds up to something that, far from being a mere round of frivolity, is positively formidable.

By the late nineteenth century, the Victorian ruling classes had worked out for themselves a system of living as intricate and all-embracing as that of any primitive society lighted on

21

by anthropologists. This system—which the Victorian middle classes followed as far as they possibly could—demonstrated at every turn its ability to accommodate birth, marriage, death, sexual morality, kinship, the social ranking-order and relations with the world outside the group. Hardly a detail was left unattended to, and almost any number of combinations and permutations was possible. Thus, the business of death, linked with that of kinship, produced a set of regulations for mourning that have never been equalled for complexity before or since. The business of ranking-order, linked with that of food, produced another set of rules—that governing precedence at the dinner-table—that was only slightly less complicated.

The sole major omission seems to have been aggression. It can, of course, be argued that the upper-class obsession with field sports represented a socially acceptable safety valve for violence; but, in the face of endless testimonies from sportsmen who protested (and still protest) that the real object of their love was the hunt rather than the kill, it is probably going too far to say that out-and-out aggressive tendencies were invariably sublimated in this manner. Self-expression through a carefully-mastered skill would be a better explanation of the attraction sport wielded. 'There is', as the invaluable *Country Life* pointed out in one of its early issues, 'a sense of satisfaction in the knowledge that the game must be searched for, that it has some chance of escape, and that in order to make even a decent bag man's skill and intelligence must be pitted against the natural instincts and wily resources of the wild-bred pheasant.'

Against this quotation, however, another should be set that dates from only twenty years before Queen Victoria's sunlit ride to St Paul's:

We don't want to fight, but by Jingo if we do
We've got the men, we've got the ships, we've got the money too.
We've fought the Bear before, and while Britons shall be true,
The Russians shall not have Constantinople.

For Top Victorians, there was no lack of outlet for combative feeling. They could stay at home and gulp with patriotic emotion, or they could go abroad with the Army and—amid conditions that quickly disillusioned the more thoughtful—fight: fight the Bear (although this particular encounter did not come off), or the Afghans, or the Zulus, or the Mahdi. Of course, 'abroad' in a wider sense was anywhere outside the upper-class palisade, so chest-thumping younger members of the ruling class did not even have to cross the Channel for an emotional work-out: to choose one example among many, it was the Life Guards who, with fixed bayonets, confronted a protest meeting of trades unionists in Parliament Square in 1887. The Guards were accompanied by four hundred policemen, three-quarters of whom were on horseback; the casualties among the trades unionists earned the event the name of Bloody Sunday.

To sum up, the uppermost sector of Victorian society lived by a set of rules that governed almost every possible social attitude and contingency. The Edwardians modified some of the details but clung to the general pattern. Their children in the period between the First and Second World Wars modified them drastically—but, for those wishing to be part of it, large fragments of the pattern survived. In a shadowy fashion, some of them still survive today.

It was around these rules that the Victorian social calendar—their annual programme for living—was constructed. Gradually, the rules fell into abeyance, but the edifice built on them has proved that it can stand perfectly well by itself. This book is an attempt to explain how, in some of its most important aspects, that programme for living was originally made to work and how the rules that underpinned it both limited the activities involved and eased them along. That they *did* ease them is obvious at every point: a Victorian woman, in the uneasy first stages of making a new friend, was supported by the card-and-call ritual; an Edwardian hostess, anxious to show the due degree of respect to each member of her dinner party, had the rules of precedence to fall back on. The upper-class father of the 1890s, paying out £1000 for the hire of a London house for the Season and £50 for each of his womenfolk's *grandes toilettes,* would naturally hope to see a return for his money. What he wanted was an advantageous match for his daughter, one that would enhance the power and prestige of his whole family; a whole system of checks and balances existed to help to ensure that something of the order would take place. No débutante, unless she were extremely headstrong or ingenious, would have a chance of ruining things by eloping with a penniless author or any other unsuitable man.

What the individual rules were will become apparent in later chapters. But they all, without exception, notched into one main super-rule of 'be controlled'. Everything, in the upper-class world of the last century, needed to be controlled, to fit into its own place or time, to proceed according to established ideas of what was suitable. Thus, the right place to be in at about 12.30 on a June Sunday was one particular spot in Hyde Park. The right time for servants' breakfast was eight o'clock; 'family' ate at nine. The right procedure for a hostess at a luncheon-party was to stimulate general conversation; in the evening she hoped that the diners would remember their conversational duties by themselves.

Within this controlled setting, expressions of individuality were allowed to flourish—but only in a controlled way. The classic example here is adultery: perfectly permissible as long as nothing 'got out' about it. The motto was not so much total secrecy as discretion. 'Have you seen Maisie?' asks Lady Charles Beresford, reported in E. F. Benson's *Mother*. 'I am told she has gone into deep mourning over Tim's death like a widow. Of course everybody knew, but she needn't remind them: so silly to dot the i's when the man's dead, and the i's have all been dotted again and again already.' The operative word here is remind: adultery was the essence of uncontrolled behaviour, and observers, however knowledgeable about the details, did not wish to be publicly, inescapably *reminded* of the basic fact.

'Reminding' those outside the palisade—the general public—was another matter again, and something to be avoided at all possible costs. Measures that in the Victorian period were taken to ward off divorce in high places included the attempted blackmail of no less a person than the Prince of Wales himself: the crown of England, the blackmailer boasted, was in his own pocket.

The boaster was Lord Randolph Churchill, who had rushed in to help in an extremely complicated struggle between his brother, Lord Blandford, his brother's mistress, Lady Aylesford, and Lady Aylesford's husband. Lord Aylesford wanted divorce; Lady Aylesford dreaded the scandal that a court case would bring on her and Blandford.

The contents of Churchill's pocket were in fact a packet of letters written to Lady Aylesford by the Prince some time earlier; Churchill hoped to use them to pressurise Edward into making Aylesford drop divorce plans. The Prince, on receiving the news, replied by asking Churchill to name his seconds. Churchill refused. The divorce was dropped in the end, and the Aylesfords separated; Churchill himself had to expiate his unprecedented effrontery by enduring eight years of social boycott.

It could be said that the most extraordinary thing about this extraordinary business was that, less than a hundred years before, the inducement represented by that packet of letters would scarcely have existed. During the early part of the nineteenth century, the sexual attachments of British Royalty were almost tediously well known by the British public. So were its debts, its gambling habits, its oddities. The Prince Regent, then the Prince of Wales, stumbled through his marriage to the awful Caroline of Brunswick in a drunken stupor. His will, written immediately after their only daughter was born, left 'all my worldly property of every description to my Maria Fitzherbert, my wife, the wife of my heart and soul'. She was also his wife in the eyes of the Church of England; his secret marriage was the cause of much speculation in Society gossip, in the press and in the House of Commons. Prinny later had Caroline tried for adultery in the House of Lords (she got off) and turned her away from Westminster Abbey when she arrived for his coronation as George IV.

Like King, like aristocracy. The Georgian ruling classes showed an equally boisterous contempt for what others thought of them. ('Others' included God: 'I don't believe a word of it,' was what Prinny's brother, the Duke of Sussex, wrote in the margin of his prayer-book.) Their aims in life were style, courage, dash; anything else was irrelevant. 'Damn your eyes, sir!' they would bawl and collapse snoring under the sideboard. That sideboard, incidentally, would be well furnished with chamber-pots; the British milord's habit of relieving himself more or less as he drank was something that had greatly shocked the polished French visitor La Rochefoucauld. Plenty of great houses accommodated a mixed brood of legitimate and natural children, on show to all comers, while the eleventh Duke of Norfolk went so far as to streamline the situation by paying all the mothers of his numerous by-blows a yearly allowance on the same day at the same bank.

If table manners in the great Georgian mansions tended to the deplorable, the sense of humour showed by their owners was often downright perilous. As late as 1834, an unnamed 'lady of title' is recorded as having combined both food and fun by taking a picnic party of seventeen to the Zoological Society's first version of Whipsnade, a farm at Kingston Hill. After an *al fresco* meal, the party set to work: they filled the animals' drinking troughs with punch, they harried the wildfowl, and, choosing the kangaroos and zebras as their quarry, they organised a hunt. View-hallooing through the establishment after two of the world's most dangerous kickers, they left the keepers with a clearing-up job that would last into the small hours.

It was this sort of uncontrolled, crazily spontaneous behaviour that the Victorian rules of conduct were expressly devised to stamp out. (The fact that the lady and her companions were obviously as drunk as lords is something that we would deprecate even today.) If, the underlying feeling went, people acted as spontaneously as that, there would be no knowing where they stood in relation to the group as a whole. And this was something that the Victorians needed to know very much.

The Hanoverian aristocrats were so grand, so self-assured, that nothing could touch them. Individuals might eat like hogs, swear like troopers and beget bastards by the score, but they were still the Duke of this, Earl of that, owners of countless acres and rulers of the country. Furthermore, there were very few of them: Britain's ruling class in the eighteenth century was composed of scarcely more than three to four hundred families whose wealth and power stemmed virtually without exception from the possession of land.

During that century, however, this number began—very slowly—to grow, thanks to wealth derived not merely from land ownership but from improved farming methods. The Napoleonic Wars, with the immense boost they gave to home-grown food production, hastened the growth still further. And the process did not stop there: from the first years of the nineteenth century onwards, 'new' wealth from land, especially from land which was suddenly needed for urban development, flooded into the upper classes, bringing newcomers to those classes with it. (Later, the flood would be augmented still further by a spate of money from industry, carrying on its tide considerable numbers of very wealthy self-made men.) At the same time, political power began to lose its hand-in-hand link with the great aristocratic families: the 1832 Reform Act brought some of that power to the upper *middle* class. By the end of the nineteenth century, the four hundred families at the top of Britain had expanded tenfold, and an alternative name for Society with a capital S was the 'Upper Ten Thousand'.

Given this continuing move up the ladder on the part of the financially and socially enterprising, it was inevitable that a sense of insecurity should develop amongst those who had just steadied themselves on a rung higher than the one they were used to, or who were about to. Not for them the flaunted mistresses and rowdy wives, the public carouses, the homeric drinking-bouts. These might be the habits of the 'old' aristocracy, but they bore an unfortunate resemblance to those of the classes that the social climber could remember all too vividly as inhabiting the ladder's lower rungs. If he fell rather than climbed, that was where he would end up. 'See how refined—therefore upper-class—I am,' was now the general message, along with its corollary, 'Are you as refined—therefore upper-class—as I?'

Gradually, set rules of 'refined' behaviour began to emerge: regular church-going and family prayers; the card-and-call ritual, which set a control on a person's approachability; the carefully-fostered horror at any suggested connections between a 'good' woman and her natural functions. The Prince Regent's daughter, Charlotte, had worn the newly-fashionable drawers and had sat with both them and her ankles showing; twenty years later, a true lady would be showing precious little of her anatomy to observers but her face. Her sexual nature, of course, had become a matter for deepest shame.

The *nouveaux riches,* energetically climbing the social ladder, took the essentially middle-class notion of gentility (itself a refined version of the ultimate social divider, 'respectability') with them. Gentility became not merely middle-class but upper-class as well. The accession of Queen Victoria in 1837 and, to an even greater extent, her marriage to the serious-minded Prince Albert in 1840 were unmistakable signs to such members of the aristocracy who still boozed and swore that they would have to mend their ways, or go under. Against newly-rich upstarts they might, to some extent, hold out, but not against a Fount of Honour who was also a newly-wed young lady: hot-tempered and lively maybe, but firmly determined to make up for an insecure childhood by embracing the middle-class ideal of blameless domesticity.

It was fashionable to be good; it was also, as its practitioners found out, surprisingly helpful. A society which has a checklist of rules to work by can use that checklist for vetting those who want to join. That they should not be allowed to join unless they were as 'good'—as refined, as upper (or upper-middle) class—as the existing members went without saying. A family which had just struggled to the top of the ladder was far more likely to feel tainted by contact with someone on a lower rung than a family whose place at the top had been assured for years. Even mere presence could taint: for that reason, those at the top took their gatherings away from the clubs such as Almacks and the pleasure gardens that the Regency bucks had frequented and located them firmly under private roofs. By the time Victoria was settled on the throne, entrance to these gatherings had become by invitation only.

If a newcomer seemed to know all the rules, invitations would, with luck, be forthcoming; he was well on the way to probationary membership, if not outright membership itself. But membership of what? The answer is not merely 'the upper classes' but that notoriously indefinable entity, Society with its capital S. Victorian Society may have consisted of the Upper Ten Thousand, but a place in it depended just as much on social prestige as on social rank. It was a plain Mrs Gardner who gave that Jubilee party in honour of the Duke of Saxe-Coburg and Gotha; it was an untitled Mr Astor who planned that 'millionaire's cheque-book' concert. Society, then, was an exclusive inner group of the upper class—but it was not so exclusive as to refuse admittance to outsiders who appeared to have something to contribute in the way of money, charm or achievement and who indicated that they understood Society's regulations. For outsiders who were forced to remain outside, it was still the accepted leader in most social matters. And, as much as anything, it was a place: a whole catalogue of places.

Being in Society meant not only being accepted by other

people who were in Society but also being present and correct at all the events that other people in Society patronised. The events themselves were none other than the fixed points of the upper classes' social calendar.

This, an ordered set of instructions on how a Society person should spend the year, was both desirable and necessary. It was in its own right one of the most important rules that the upper classes ever drew up to control gatecrashers. And its beginnings were surprisingly practical. Until comparatively recently, Parliament met from February to August, at which point the smell of the Thames made London insupportable. The Hanoverian lord liked to mix business with pleasure: every year, he and his family would make the trip to the capital, intent on a short whirl of social festivities that would have to last them until the next annual visit fell due. The Victorians took over this habit and added further embellishments. By the end of the nineteenth century, the London Season was fixed in all its details, as was the rest of the yearly programme. The Season was followed by a short spell at the sea or watering-place; those who had taken part in the London social whirl—and to do this properly was an arduous job—needed recuperation. Then came what was for many the most important business of the year: sport. There was a migration to Scotland and Yorkshire for grouse in August and another to the hunting shires in November. For all but those directly connected with government, early spring presented a lull—but a solution to boredom could be found abroad. Winter and early spring became the season for the South of France. Then April came round again: the New Year of the national social calendar, and the starting-point for ten thousand individual social calendars of parties, marriages, visits, race-meetings, festivals of the Church, dress-fittings, charity bazaars and encounters with the bicycle or, late in the period, the horseless victoria.

The progression of events that the social calendar prescribed, expensive and time-consuming as they were, formed an ideal instrument for separating the social sheep from the goats. A truly 'arrived' person would be present at such-and-such a dinner, such-and-such a shoot or houseparty or ball. A person whose 'arrival' was still in the future would not. He (or she) would still need to expend considerable time, determination and money before the invitations to the really exclusive events would start to come in; it might indeed be a process that spanned a whole generation, if not two. But, in addition to this vital but concealed function, the social calendar had other, more obvious ones. In the early Victorian period at least, it provided a setting in which the upper classes could continue to exercise their still immense political power outside the Palace of Westminster. (An alternative to the social calendar was, of course, the club. The Carlton was the premier club for Tories, the Reform for Liberals; by the end of the nineteenth century there were over a hundred others, catering for all types of political and temperamental persuasion.) It also, and very importantly, provided a framework in which young people's gatherings could be arranged and supervised. The acquisition—under carefully controlled circumstances—of fiancés for Society daughters was one of the London Season's acknowledged ends.

There was also what might be thought the very simple question of straightforward entertainment. But, as it turns out, it was by no means straightforward. The men, certainly, enjoyed hunting, shooting and fishing and always had. The ladies had the Season's more formalised pleasures; indeed, all social intercourse of the drawing-room variety, in Season or out, was very much a matter of 'ladies' game'. But many of them, men and women, approached this year-long programme of self-indulgence in a spirit not so much of gleeful anticipation as of selfless submission to some higher end.

True, the real butterflies of Society didn't give a hoot about the moral niceties of their actions. But the more thoughtful members of the upper classes went through the social round convinced that they were fulfilling a threefold duty. They had, first, a duty to their families. They also had a duty to their class as a whole; upper-class solidarity is a considerably older phenomenon than its working-class equivalent. And then they had a duty to the millions outside the palisade who, it was felt, could not help but admire their betters and, in admiring, learn.

'Without an aristocracy,' commented the French historian and critic Hippolyte Taine, who made several visits to mid-Victorian Britain and wrote about the experiences in his invaluable *Notes on England*, 'a civilisation is not complete; it wants large, independent lives, emancipated from all mean care, capable of beauty like a work of art. . . . [The aristocracy] maintains certain elegancies of manners and certain shades of sentiments, renders possible a cosmopolitan education, supplies a hotbed for statesmen.' For many representatives of the group he was describing, the first two attributes would have presented the limit of their ambitions, though they lived up to them thoroughly. In a familiar phrase, they 'had a position to keep up'. Their clothes, food, houses, methods of transport and entertainment were all evidence of that position: evidence brought both to impress their social equals and, in a way that now seems the height of arrogance, to provide moral uplift and mental stimulus to their social inferiors. In a society that put a premium on individual hard work and struggle, they represented the most distant, dizzying, almost abstract peaks of reward. In another familiar phrase, 'they had an example to set'.

Self-justification? Possibly; indeed, probably—although of an unconscious sort. The eighteenth-century lords were not overmuch bothered about the moral impact made by the spectacle of their enjoyment; they just got on with it and enjoyed themselves. For them, the aim of living up to their position was to wipe the eye of their neighbours. It was the newcomers to the ruling classes, sensitive as to their origins and deportment and imbued with a middle-class morality, who appear to have invented the idea of doing the lower classes good. They contrived on almost every front to put up defences against those classes—defences which, however, had strategically-placed entrances through which new recruits might file—but they were not quite proof against the enemy within. The final brick needed in the bastions of upper-class solidarity was the assurance that the parties and shoots and new dresses were not merely means to pleasure but means to a dimly-apprehended greater good.

It took one world war to shake that particular assurance and another to make even its memory a matter for disbelieving contempt. But the bastions as a whole were strongly built; let us consider their architecture in detail.

CHAPTER THREE

∝∾∾

Friends

Membership of a particular class is displayed by acts which impress other like-minded persons with the suitability and likeableness of one's general manner. 'One of our sort,' they think.

Professor T. H. Pear,
English Social Differences, 1955

The Victorians, despite or possibly because of their constant strivings towards super-gentility, relished a good tale of terror. They took blood, torture and demon-lovers in their stride; the sex interest—usually represented by maidens of delicious vulnerability—was a discreet but almost invariable factor in the potpourri. Favourite sources of inspiration, even in 'respectable' magazines, were the Middle Ages at their Gothic worst and a vampire-haunted Middle Europe of an indeterminate period.

But the authors of this sub-literature were also capable of ringing the changes on contemporary themes. Among their offerings in this category is a tale that, while now needing plentiful footnotes, would have spoken straight to the hearts of all those for whom it was originally intended. Its main characters are a newly-wed wife and her jealous husband; the pivot on which the whole thing turns is the social practice of leaving cards on a household as an intimation of friendship.

The husband, obsessive in his jealousy, hides these tokens of esteem as they come in; the wife, believing that the whole world to which she has a right of social entry is ostracising her, comes close to losing her reason. And then she finds out what's been going on. For a conclusion, the story shifts from psychodrama to plain blood-and-thunder: the distraught heroine, confronted with such a plot, seeks vengeance in poisoning its perpetrator.

The basic premise on which this apparently unlikely

romance rests is, by contrast, all too accurate. Most upper- and middle-class Victorian women—and all, certainly, who numbered themselves among the Upper Ten Thousand— would have felt profoundly uneasy if the weekly quota of cards in the tray on the hall table had started to fall. If it dwindled to vanishing point, the would-be hostess's emotions would have flared into pure panic. Did people think she was away? Was her husband in social, financial or professional disgrace—and she the last to know about it? Above all, *what had she done wrong?*

Assuming that, like the unhappy lady of the story, she had done nothing wrong at all, a feeling of total unreality would have enveloped her. Not only had she suddenly been deprived of her friends, her social allies, her colleagues in what was as much her work as her husband's inscrutable doings at club or Palace of Westminster were his; she had also been confronted with a complete breakdown of the machinery that made her social and 'business' life possible. If, in the nineteenth century, your domestic and sexual reputation was unassailable, and your husband's social rank and income above a certain level (the details here were variable; the final degree and figure depended on the circles in which you wished to move), you were assured of a group of acquaintances with whom you could mix without feelings of social unease or constraint. You might not like all of them—but, for better or worse, you were one of them, free to express even your antipathies in terms that would be understood and acted upon in the correct manner. And the means whereby this state of affairs was achieved was the card-and-call system: a system open to participation by anybody who understood its rules and one which invariably produced some results, however disappointing in quality. For it to produce no results whatsoever was impossible. If, for some reason, the 'impossible' actually happened, the resulting nervous breakdown on the part of the victim would have been not only likely but justified.

The formal 'morning' call (so named because it took place before dinner, once a midday fixture) was the follow-up to the card; together, they indicated that a state of friendship existed between the two parties concerned, ready to be built upon as might seem convenient or pleasurable. Without them few other fixtures on an individual's social calendar could take place; nor would the damage have stopped there.

A best-selling etiquette-book of the turn of the century has this to say on the matter:

> The ceremony of paying calls has been ridiculed and derided during the course of many, many years as meaningless, useless, and stupid; but it is still in existence, and is as much practised as ever. Visits of form, of which most people complain, and yet to which most people submit, are absolutely necessary—being, in fact, the basis on which that great structure, society, mainly rests. You cannot invite people to your house, however often you may have met them elsewhere, until you have first called upon them in a formal manner, and they have returned the visit. It is a kind of safeguard against any acquaintances which are thought undesirable.

A warning is added, however, that the seal of approval represented by 'calling status' is not a once and for all affair. 'If you do not wish to continue the friendship,' the writer points out, 'you discontinue to call, and that is considered as an intimation of such intentions, and therefore no further advances are made by [the acquaintance]. But it would be considered very bad manners, and very uncourteous behaviour, not to return a call in the first instance.'

The author of that advice, Lady Colin Campbell, wrote—or rather revised—it in 1911, when the sales of her *Etiquette of Good Society* had come near to reaching the hundred thousand mark. (It had been published for the first time almost twenty years earlier.) The implication of such a total is clear: over ninety thousand people—mainly, one would guess, women—had begun at some point in their lives to aspire to a social standing slightly above the one to which they were used and had wanted to find out how they could set about turning aspiration into reality.

Among the complications they had to master was the intricate ritual of leaving cards and calling. Lady Colin devotes nine pages to it: to the need for paying calls on a bride, on a new mother, on new arrivals in a country neighbourhood (in towns, this needed to be preceded by an introduction); on givers of hospitality; on your friends when you returned to their area after an absence; on the sick or bereaved. The latter were characterised by much delicacy of feeling: 'sufficient time should be allowed to the family before we venture to ask to see them . . . . To ensure this respect, it has become the custom to "return thanks for kind inquiries" and after these have been received, then the call may be paid.'

Lady Colin points out that, as a rule, men do not become involved in paying visits of ceremony but adds that, if they do, they should not take their hat, stick or umbrella into the drawing-room with them. (This is, however, a new fashion; earlier usage insisted that men should keep their impedimenta with them during the call, to stress the fleeting nature of their visit.) She explains that silver-edged wedding cards are now seldom sent but that cards bearing the initials PDA or PPC *(pour dire adieu* and *pour prendre congé)* are both fashionable and correct for a card-leaver who is also about to leave the neighbourhood.

She also deals with the actual card-leaving process itself:

A lady leaves her own and two of her husband's—one is intended for the gentleman of the house and one for the lady. If a call is made upon a guest staying at the house, a card is also left for her. A lady when leaving cards for her husband must place them upon the hall table, and not leave them in the drawing-room on her departure, as was the custom. It is not usual now to turn down the corners of cards, this custom formerly involving much needless fuss and rules of etiquette. [A turned-down corner on a card indicated that the visitor had left it in person, with a view to calling, rather than having it sent round by a servant.] Cards with inquiries should be left at the door; the post is a permissible channel for the transmission of these where the distance is inconveniently great.

What Lady Colin—perhaps surprisingly—does not touch on are the complications that faced the social aspirant wanting to work up an acquaintanceship (especially an acquaintanceship of a higher social standing) from scratch. From Macclesfield to Mayfair, the rules governing this part of the operation were the same, and so were the pitfalls involved. These, at every stage of the business, were awful. The Mayfair contender had a slight advantage in her presumably easier access to knowledge of the latest nuances of behaviour—but then the social sub-group she wished to enter would also possess that knowledge, possibly to an even greater degree than the aspirant herself. In the end, nothing divided the lady of provincial society and her metropolitan sister except the nature of the social stakes played for and the enforced choice of battleground. Both needed adroitness, a fair degree of luck and an iron refusal to be unnerved.

Generally, the jumping-off point in the procedure was the introduction, effected according to the rules that are still current today: men introduced to women, the social inferior to the social superior. Without this formal bringing-together, no further developments could take place, since the parties involved had not had their meeting socially ratified. (There were occasional exceptions to the rule, but it was always up to the person of higher rank to implement them.) And, even if the aspirant managed to organise things so that she and her target acquaintance were in the same place at the same time, with a willing friend hovering with the words 'May I present . . .' on her lips, the target still had to give her own permission for the introduction to take place. True, the friend might stage-manage the encounter so that refusal would appear churlish, but this would be, if repeated too often, a passport to definite social demotion. If, however, the target did give way, however grudgingly, the aspirant could count herself in a position to start the game in earnest.

It opened with further by-play in public: encounters at charity bazaars, in the Park (or its provincial equivalent) or in drawing-rooms. In all of them, the target (we are assuming throughout that she was of higher social status than her pursuer) had the initiative. If the aspirant received a bow of greeting, a smile or actual conversation, the game could go on; with luck these evidences of interest might develop in time into the appearance of cards bearing the names of the target and her husband on the hall table. There would have been no enquiry as to whether the aspirant was at home, but that didn't matter. The time for enquiries came later.

If the target's cards did appear, the aspirant would return her own within a week; the vital preliminaries thus completed, the way would soon be open for calls. Alternatively, the aspirant could take matters into her own hands by initiating the card-leaving ceremony herself. For the time being, she was safe, since the target was almost certain to obey the rule that cards must be left in return; but if, emboldened, the aspirant followed up with a call and *still* received cards in return, the message was painfully obvious. Its meaning, as an 1893 issue of The Lady points out, is that the card-leaver 'did not desire the acquaintance to ripen into friendship'. (Strict etiquette, the journal goes on to say, demands that a call should be returned by a call and a card by a card.)

That such a snub should have had to be made at all was an indication that the target's social poise—and therefore standing—was perhaps less absolute than her would-be acquaintance thought it was. There were recognised ways of indicating, well before the cards stage was reached, that an introduction was to remain undeveloped. The 'cut' consisted of, variously, the coolest of greetings, a refusal to let eyes meet, a stony and unresponsive stare and a stately progress across the street to the opposite pavement. All four methods were, of necessity, administered in public; by today's lights, they sound both heartless and, in the case of the last variant, abominably rude. But their recipient, however mortified by the experience, would not have agreed; she would have been equally ready to use the 'cut' herself if circumstances demanded and would have felt quite justified in doing so. Like the card-and-call ritual itself, the cut was an accepted part of the game. (Interestingly, it was a part in which women had a definite advantage over men. 'A gentleman', says Lady Colin, 'must not either bow or shake hands with a lady until she has made the first movement, neither must he, under any circumstances, fail to return her courtesies.')

But suppose that our aspirant has weathered all the early hazards of making a new friend; that she has exercised enough self-control to let her target take the first moves every step of the way; that, on the occasion of the target's first call, the flowers had been fresh, the conversation had stuck firmly to trivialities and no offer of tea had been made. (Tea-parties, as the aspirant knows, are in the realms of 'by invitation only' and thus several stages further into intimacy than a visit of ceremony.) She has certainly been accepted, but there is still one obstacle to be faced: her return call on the person she cautiously thinks of as a friend. She will now be asked to display all the social *savoir faire* she possesses: in all likelihood, she will also be meeting the friend's own social circle, and she will have to please, therefore, in not one direction but several. Furthermore, she will have only fifteen minutes in which to do it. A quarter of an hour is the absolute maximum for a formal visit; less would be polite if other callers are already present.

At mid-afternoon on the chosen day, the call-payer goes

into action. Whatever happens, the whole thing must be over and done with before five o'clock; after that time, visits fall into the 'between intimate friends' category, and the caller knows she is nowhere near that stage yet. When her victoria arrives at its destination, the caller gives her card to her servant, who then hands it in at the door. The piece of pasteboard is taken upstairs to the lady of the house, who on seeing it will decide whether to receive its owner. The caller, meanwhile, is combining an appearance of calm dignity with a certain breathlessness. The message finally comes back: the mistress is At Home. The caller mounts the steps, ignores the card-tray on the hall table (her husband's cards will be given to her own or her hostess's servant at the *end* of the visit) and enters the drawing-room. Any men present will rise to greet her, as will the hostess; the ladies stay where they are. The visitor is introduced round the circle, seats herself—as is correct—on the nearest vacant chair to the hostess and discovers that conversation is about, say, opera.

With her internal stopwatch set for ten minutes, she waits for her moment, collects her wits and finally indicates that she, too, loves *Tristan*. The ladies round her allow themselves to feel a faint flicker of approval; the hostess, sensing it, would feel a corresponding flicker of relief. She, after all, is now in the position of introducer and carries the social responsibility for her discovery.

What are they looking for, these established members of the circle? Up to a point, certainly, they are on the watch for evidence of personal congeniality. If the visitor had owned that she positively hated *Tristan*, she would have dampened any sense of fellow-feeling among Wagner lovers present. But, at the same time, she would have made a far more fundamental mistake: so strong an expression of dislike does not fall into the categories of conversation considered suitable for a formal call. By its very nature, it is controversial—its originator runs the risk of starting an argument, upsetting the social apple cart. Above all, she would have given an affirmative answer to the question her observant fellow-callers most needed answering: *would the newcomer make people feel awkward?*

Obviously, the ways in which people might be made to feel awkward varied from class to class and circle to circle. A few main headings can, however, be extracted from the morass. They are: lack of an acceptable moral (we would say sexual) reputation; lack of required family background; lack of wealth (which might or might not be synonymous with hard ready cash; a 'good' background would, however, make up for considerable relative poverty); lack of assurance; and lack of ability—whether stemming from temperament or ignorance—to conform to the group's social demands.

To be truly accepted into a new circle, the visitor has to prove that she lacks nothing in all five respects; to score a bad mark on any one of them would be to show oneself as a walking reminder that things in that quiet drawing-room might suddenly run out of control. Since her very presence there, however, indicates that her background, good name and financial status have already been found acceptable by her hostess, her observers can now concentrate on the other points. They will listen to her voice (too shrill? too breathy? a trace of undesirable accent?) and pay attention, not just to what she says, but to how she says it. Does she say 'father' rather than the correct 'my father?' Does she gush? Does she wear the right clothes for the occasion, does she move without flurrying, does she keep her gestures to a minimum? Above all, does she carry herself with a poise that declares that she is neither the group's superior nor yet its hopeful probationer but a potential full member as of right?

Within fifteen minutes, a judgment will have been made; in some cases five will have been enough. Within ten, the caller in question will rise gracefully to her feet, murmur goodbye to her hostess and leave. Her husband's cards are given to her servant, who again climbs the steps to the portico to hand them in. The caller sinks back in her carriage, ruffles her pet dog's ears (the animal was left in the victoria for the duration; dogs and children are not admitted to drawing-rooms) and considers that it all went well enough.

It continues to go well enough; further calls are made and returned, the former target's card becomes a familiar sight in the aspirant's card-basket, and she is slowly absorbed into the new circle. The target's friends initiate card-and-call moves of their own; one invitation to a tea is followed by another. Then—triumph—there is an invitation to a dinner party. The aspirant has been put through one of the most delicate screening systems ever devised by a social group to protect its integrity and has survived the ordeal. Barring accidents and calumny, she is home and dry—until she decides to scale some further heights.

CHAPTER FOUR

∽∾∽

Gatherings

It is the ambition of the modern woman to show herself everywhere.

E. C. Grenville Murray,
Side-lights on English Society, 1881

Amongst both the Top Victorians and their humbler imitators, a young girl's future was usually mapped out in the drawing-rooms frequented by her mother. To a lesser but still distinguishable degree, a man's career could be made or broken by his wife's skill at amassing five o'clock contacts. It was the women of the upper and upper-middle classes who held the invitations to dinners, musical evenings, receptions, garden parties and balls in their tightly-gloved grasp. At all these, attendant males might be brought into circles that would otherwise have stayed closed to them, while daughters doing their first, second or—to their quiet desperation—third Season might find a beau whose affections proved durable. It was possible, of course, to encounter beaux in the drawing-rooms themselves, especially on Sundays; Sunday afternoon was the recognised time for calls from either family members or unmarried men (the latter were said to be 'sowing seeds'). But, by and large, the drawing-rooms were pre-eminently the preserve of the senior women: their places of business ('If *we* have our dinner on the 15th, that will fit in with both your dance and Millie's *soirée*'); their clearing-houses of information ('Jane's son is coming along very well'); their tribunals of justice against which there was no appeal ('Poor dear Henry—so *sad*'). For all their apparent docility in the 1840s, frivolity in the 1870s and gorgeous empty-headedness in the 1900s, the female upholders of the social calendar could wield immense power over their group while seldom appearing at the events that the calendar featured.

But such appearances were obviously something that only the shyest, dottiest or most elderly amongst them would dream of passing up. Not to join in the public social round would mean forgoing the delights of seeing one's power put into effect. In addition, and just as important, there was the question of upper-class solidarity or 'duty'. An upper class that did not publicly live in an upper-class way was failing in its duty—and, during the London Season, duty took a remarkable number of forms.

There were the charity meetings and bazaars, the carriage drives and—of course—the calls; the visits to the Zoo, to the Botanical Gardens in Regent's Park, to Hurlingham and Richmond; the garden parties, private views and afternoon concerts; the musical evenings and receptions, the full-scale balls. Provincial society, with its more restricted opportunities, followed suit as best it might. (As eager as its London equivalent to bestow an air of exclusivity on its activities, it insisted that county balls, though they were run on an 'admission by subscription' basis, should be open only to subscribers bearing an introduction from a third party known to the ball's stewards or patroness.) London and its surroundings also offered the more 'public' grand occasions like the Opera, the theatre and the great sporting fixtures such as Ascot and Henley. The latter, together with Society's main participatory sports, will be dealt with later; to get some idea of how the main non-sporting gatherings on the upper-class social calendar were conducted, let us start with its entries for good works.

The concept of good works now carries heavy overtones of self-righteousness. It is important to stress, therefore, that this was something that would and could never have occurred to a responsibly-minded lady of Victorian or Edwardian Society. To her mind, there was nothing wrong at all with being a Lady Bountiful, with patronising charitable organisations, with allowing her daughters to play shopkeeper at charity bazaars. (The point here, of course, was that it was play only—and the objects sold were, as the children's writer E. Nesbit neatly sums up, 'table-covers and mats and things embroidered beautifully by idle ladies with no real work to do'.)

Good works were, indeed, a line of action in which royalty itself gave the lead. Queen Victoria visited hospitals and made baskets—rather unsaleable ones—for bazaars; cheering her wounded soldiers, she wrote in her journal, was 'one of the *few* agreeable privileges of our position and it

certainly *pays* us for many disagreeable ones'. Queen
Alexandra, in her turn, was a lavish contributor to charity;
during one of her hospital visits, she delighted an injured
soldier by twitching up her petticoats and swinging her lame
leg over his bedside table. 'My dear, dear man,' she told him,
'I hear you have a stiff leg; so have I. Now just watch what I
can do with it.'

It is doubtful, however, whether the Society ladies
following the royal example ever brought Victoria's level of
feeling or Alexandra's spontaneity to their task. Certainly,
until the First World War brought even the most refined of
volunteers into contact with gangrene, farm work, factories
and the world outside the drawing-room in general, only the
exceptionally dedicated and strong-minded 'charity workers'
from the upper classes came in close, sustained contact with
those whom they hoped to help. Work in an East End
settlement would naturally bring on the dreaded 'awkward'
feeling to excess: how could a hatted, gloved, boa-ed and
thoroughly pampered lady of the '90s feel anything less
when faced with the Other London?

No; what Society ladies liked was the controlled degree of
involvement implied, for example, by the following
description of a self-help institute for the genteelly poor. The
institute was

> under the patronage of the Duchess of Sutherland, the
> Dowager Countess of Dunmore, the Marchioness of
> Westminster, the Marchioness Townsend, the Dowager
> Countess of Westmorland, the Lady Anne Sherson, the
> Lady Henniker, and Mrs Self; and under the super-
> intendance of Mrs Una Howard. The promoters of this
> institution seek to place within the reach of educated
> ladies, widows, and daughters of clergymen, barristers,
> military and naval officers, and professional men, who
> may have been reduced from easy circumstances to
> narrow means, an opportunity of turning their natural or
> acquired abilities to account. Rooms have been opened at
> the premises, Bessborough-gardens [sic], for the recep-
> tion and sale of articles produced by ladies in reduced
> circumstances. These rooms are now crowded with a great
> variety of articles of every description—oil paintings,
> drawings, modelled waxwork, guipure and other lace,
> wool-work, embroidery, baby-clothes, and plain work of

all sorts. Although the institution has been established but a very short time, and although its funds are yet limited, over 383 receipts have been given out for work.

The receipts came from the ladies who showed their charitable intentions by patronising Bessborough Gardens; it is clear that, even though the objects of charity are in this case ladies themselves, there was absolutely no need for the charitably intent to come face to face with them. That too, of course, could have been 'awkward'.

The above details were collected (from, one feels, the institution's own hand-out) by a Turk called Azamat Batuk, who visited Great Britain in the late 1860s. In between his fact-finding ventures into the upper-class world, he published his impressions in the *Pall Mall Gazette*. His fair readers—if any; he did not pull his punches—would have winced at his subsequent remarks on the charitable institute's stock-in-trade. 'This kind of productions,' he said, 'if they are good, do not want to go to Bessborough Gardens to be sold; and if they are not good, nobody wants them.'

Worse, in a more subtle way, was to come. Mr Batuk had been present at the institute's annual general meeting.

After a considerable amount of eloquence had been expended and the annual report read, several powdered footmen arrived with large silver trays full of cups of coffee, tea, of various cakes, and of little jugs of cream. This last delicacy excited general admiration from the ladies; while the gentlemen were chiefly engaged in looking for Mr Gladstone, probably, with a view to present him their compliments. Unhappily, however, the great statesman disappeared just before the speeches were brought to a close.

This, obviously, was one occasion when the Society ploy of making contacts for one's menfolk did not come off.

An upper-class lady would have regarded an afternoon such as this as rigorous work. The job of listening to the 'considerable amount of eloquence'—most of it on topics either abstract or completely outwith her experience—would have left her with the satisfaction of a hard job done. A more familiar task, and part of her overall duty of seeing and being seen in public, was the regular deployment of herself, her

daughters, her carriage, her horses and her footmen in that
section of her neighbourhood appointed by usage for the
purpose. In London, this was Hyde Park.

Biographer and historian Percy Colson, who was
twenty-nine when Queen Victoria died, recalled during the
Second World War the Society scene of his youth.

In the afternoon it was *de rigueur* to drive on the
Knightsbridge side of the Park. There the carriageway
would present an almost solid phalanx of victorias,
barouches, and landaus, all with coachmen and footmen,
many of them powdered. In them sat elaborately dressed
and *coiffured* women and their daughters, *les jeunes filles
à marier.* Up and down they drove for the regulation
number of turns, bowing to their friends and trying to
look as if they were enjoying themselves. Women not
quite in the swim trying to look as if they were; in the
seventh heaven if someone belonging to the inner circle
gave them a careless half-bow.

The congestion was frightful. A much earlier
commentator described it as a 'strange notion of the pleasure
of a drive; with the carriages in a close line jammed all
together, and sometimes coming to a dead stop like the
omnibuses in Fleet Street of an afternoon, and seldom
moving on faster than mourning coaches at a funeral'. An
alternative was to stroll or sit on the chairs the Park
provided—an alternative that was itself *de rigueur* on
Sundays, when Society, prayer book in hand, filled in the
time between church and luncheon by seeing and letting
itself be seen in the neighbourhood of Stanhope Gate.

Further west and south were other alternatives still which,
like Hyde Park drive itself, were all established early on in
our period. In 1849, observer and writer Percival Leigh
turned his attention to several and wrote them up in a
straining imitation of Samuel Pepys; it was, however, a
technique well suited to his subject.

Here, for example, is his account of Kensington Gardens,
where a Guards band played every Friday and Monday
through the Season.

The tunes played mostly polkas and waltzes, though now
and then an excuse for a number of people assembling to
see and be seen .... Many [beauties] in seats with tall

well-looking gallants posted beside them, or bending
down to converse with them with vast attention and
politeness, whereat they seeming mightily pleased. Others
standing in groups here and there under the shade, and a
great throng of them round about the musicians; but all
walking to and fro between the tunes to show themselves.
Many of the Army among the crowd, and strange, to
compare them and others of our gentry, in air and
manner, with one or two dingy foreigners with their great
beards and ill-favoured looks. The little fashionable
children by the side of their mammas elegant enough to
see; but overdressed in their velvet and plaid tunics and
plumes of feathers, and their ways too mincing and
dainty, and looking as though they had stepped from out
of a band-box.

At the flower show at Chiswick Gardens it was the same
story: the sun shone, the band played, the visitors admired
the orchids, azaleas, cacti, pelargoniums, roses and each
other. The latter-day Pepys, meanwhile, owned to qualms
lest any acquaintance in the carriages arriving should have
seen him getting out of an omnibus.

Mr Leigh also visited the Zoo, on the non-exclusive day of
Monday. Sunday was the day when Society promenaded on
the brand-new Terrace, contemplated the tigers and the
bears climbing their pole for buns and—when faced with its
newly-arrived namesake—hummed the tune of the
fashionable 'Hippopotamus Polka'. (The poor hippo, though
the favourite of London, had rather a sad time at first: he
was so scared of the large pool built for him that he wouldn't
go in unless accompanied by his keeper. Queen Victoria,
herself a great animal-lover, was much impressed by the
trusting relationship between them.)

All the activities mentioned so far have been daytime ones,
ones at which the presence of a man, though useful and
pleasurable, was not absolutely necessary. A young girl
would be accompanied by her mother, aunt or chaperon;
senior ladies could, if they wished, accompany each other.
But there was another group of events which would have
been dreariness itself without the male element—the daytime
parties. Garden parties, picnics, the various gatherings
centred round lawn sports, boating parties—they all offered
opportunities to see and be seen in charmingly informal

settings. And they all gave the débutante a chance to meet the opposite sex under conditions less restrictive than those of the ballroom. As Mary, Countess of Lovelace, commented in an anthology of recollections spanning the years 1882 to 1932:

> Opportunities for young people to mingle freely in peaceful country surroundings had to be provided more or less by some hostess, who presided. The best of these, I think, were water parties, say, of a dozen people at most, who spent long hours boating on the river, eating and resting at intervals in some little waterside inn. There used to be a place of the sort called 'Skindle's' at Maidenhead, which was a home of delight to many of us. I think that expenses were often pooled. The chaperonage which the modern young person visualizes as such a bug-a-boo was on these occasions provided usually by some one kindly matron, 'somebody's mother', who was willing to sit long hours in the sun watching other people's amusements.

(Skindles Hotel by the river is, of course, still going strong.)

At night, however, formality returned with a rush. At the height of the London Season, when three or four balls were given every night except Saturday (the need to finish by midnight was the cause of this abstention), the most restful way to spend an evening was seated in full evening dress and diamonds in the stalls, the dress circle or a box at Covent Garden. Opera was Society's oldest, most important and in many cases only cultural love; 'good society', wrote Hippolyte Taine as late as the 1860s, 'does not go to the theatres, with the exception of the two opera houses, which are the exotic and hot-house plants of luxury, and in which the prices of admission are enormous.' The opening night of the Covent Garden season was one of the earliest landmarks of the Season itself, and members of Society treated the place as if it were their own.

Vita Sackville-West, in her classic work of semi-fiction, *The Edwardians*, describes what happened:

> Upper circles and gallery were full; the stalls and boxes but sparsely occupied. Into the stalls, people trickled in parties of two and four, tiptoeing in the semi-darkness; into the boxes, parties came with less circumspection,

having no resentful feet to stumble over, no whispered apologies to make; they came in, with a gleam of light as the door opened, and took their places amid scarcely suppressed chatter and laughter. Sh-sh-sh, came from the circles and gallery, but the disturbers glanced round, although unseen, into the dim amphitheatre as though chidden by an intruder in their own home. As the first act wore on, these gleamings and rustlings diminished and subsided; the stalls filled up; and the house began to await the final chords of the orchestra and the turning-up of the lights, when the full splendour of Covent Garden should be revealed.

By this period, the theatre—once regarded as thoroughly unfashionable, even unrespectable—had caught up. In the last decades of the old century, London had been thrilled to the core by plays like *The Second Mrs Tanqueray*, starring Stella Campbell, and *Trilby*, with Sir Herbert Tree as Svengali. But music halls, the most vital form of British theatre art then existing, still presented complications. They were no places for young ladies—less because of the content of the show (which had, in any case, grown immeasurably in sophistication since its penny gaff beginnings of Dickens' time) than because of those who attended it. The most popular music hall of them all, the Empire, was frequented by some of the best-bred men in the land: 'to be "chucked out of the Empire" was part of the worldly experience of every gilded youth,' commented social and fashion historian James Laver; 'it is amusing to reflect that this fate once overtook no less a person than Winston Churchill.' And a married woman, well protected by her male relatives, might occupy one of its boxes. But the promenade area at the back of the stalls was frequented by the *other* Ladies of the Empire. Members of the highest class of whores, they dressed, moved and behaved exquisitely; a breach of decorum would have led to their expulsion from the house. Their presence, though, brought frequent and frantic protests from the righteous. Morals apart, the emotions behind those protests are easily understood: for a 'good' woman to be under the same roof as an openly-acknowledged tart was a classic case for awkwardness, and for that tart to be on an equal level of finery and self-assurance brought the 'good' woman's feelings of insecurity and discomfort to unbearable heights. (As always, though, there were the occasional exceptions to the rule. Lady de Grey, Colson recalls, was the 'unquestioned leader of the smart opera set and an intimate friend of the Prince [of Wales]'. She also once had the intoxicating experience of being the subject of an attempted pick-up at the Monte Carlo casino. 'The woman who was with her was furious,' Colson goes on, 'but she herself was charmed and exclaimed delightedly: "He takes me for a *cocotte:* I was never so flattered!" ')

Music halls, then, might be dubious; but ordinary music and Society were generally accepted as being perfect partners. Better still: throwing a private concert, with the help of one or more of the musical idols of the moment, was an excellent way of boosting both one's social status and one's tally of acquaintances. A top Society lady might have grave doubts about attending her social inferior's ball; she would have few about an evening adorned by Melba, Caruso, Christine Nilsson. As a social ploy, however, the grand private concert did not come cheap—Melba alone cost five hundred guineas a performance—and there was the added complication of deciding just where, on the social ladder, the performers stood.

That this problem, together with the difficulties posed by the whole amateur v. professional question, lasted well into the twentieth century is shown by some advice given in a 'textbook of hospitality' written in the 1930s by June and Doris Langley Moore, *The Pleasure of Your Company*. The authors warn that what they are going to say may be superfluous, but it clearly was not so even a few years before.

> You must receive entertainers of standing as if they were your guests, and treat them with the consideration due to guests. Musicians are no longer kept waiting in an ante-room until it is time for them to appear, nor do they, unless they wish it, have their refreshments served to them separately, and go home as soon as they have eaten supper.

And there is another point.

> Incidentally, you must take care how you ask professional artists to oblige you in an amateur capacity. You have no more right to assume that a concert pianist should be

willing to provide nocturnes and sonatas gratis for your guests than that your florist, if invited, should apply free decorations. There is an old story of a famous violinist who, being invited to come to dinner and bring his violin, replied, 'Thank you, but my violin never dines.'

The rebuke, the Langley Moores add, was well deserved; its originator was probably the Spanish virtuoso Sarasate, who once refused to play before the Prince of Wales without first making sure of his hundred guineas' fee.

Musical attractions such as this were a usual—but not inevitable—component of one of the three ultra-grand ways of filling a Society evening in the London Season. The Victorians called this a reception, a 'kettledrum' (or 'drum') or a *soirée*; between-the-wars socialites moved it further back in the day's timetable and turned it into a cocktail party; today, amongst all those who are past the disco age, it is synonymous with the word 'party' itself. The main common denominators of all three are that dancing is not expected and that the event is attended by as many people as can be secured and squashed into the space allotted.

Nineteenth-century guests at a reception of this sort did not necessarily expect to meet, still less to talk to, their friends; at a really good 'drum' the crush would be too great. You were announced, given token welcome by your hosts and left to your own devices. Here is Percival Leigh, still in the style of Pepys, at a mid-Season *soirée* in a titled home (he is not sure whether he and his host have ever met but ascribes his invitation to his name being in the *Court Guide*).

Surely there was something worth seeing and hearing; but saw nothing extraordinary beyond the multitude of company, and divers writers, painters, and other persons of note, elbowing their way through the press; nor heard anything but puffing and gasping and complaining of the terrible heat. Several ladies fainting; and my wife declaring she should faint too . . . . At some distance before us, a bustle and stir, and in the midst of it a lackey with a tray, whereon were ices—the people struggling for them; and I also strove to get one for my wife and myself as well; but the attempt vain, and we borne clear away by the current to the other side of the room; and in the mean time all the ice must have melted.

The Leighs, unsurprisingly, left early, 'mighty proud that I had been invited by my Lord, though utterly tired with his party,' Percival concluded, summing up one of the main factors that kept the social calendar ticking over.

Dances were grander, more formal and better organised, while grandest of all was the full-scale ball, which was a dance on the largest, most lavish scale possible. Between them, Lady Colin Campbell and the Langley Moores give a clear idea of what, over the span of forty years, giving a dance meant in practical terms. Lady Colin stresses that at least six or seven rooms should be set aside for the event: 'two cloak-rooms, tea and refreshment room, drawing-room for the reception, ball-room, card and supper rooms'. The Langley Moores, writing in a period when available house-space had shrunk drastically, suggest that a hotel is probably the best venue—although, as they point out, it 'has been *à la mode* during the last few years to take a large empty house for one night, and fill it with sufficient hired furniture, carpets, and curtains, and so forth, to give an appearance of festive grandeur'. But this procedure, they add, involves more trouble than it is worth.

Lady Colin lays great stress on flowers: 'There cannot be too great a display . . . . The fireplaces should be screened with them or with large ferns, so filled as to resemble a garden bank. The mantelpieces may be covered with small tin trays, containing flowers. Console tables, or any other flat surface, may be decorated in like manner; and on the staircase, below the banister, flowers are often arranged so as to appear as if growing there.' The Langley Moores, curiously, do not mention them. But nor does Lady Colin give any advice in the order of the suggestion from the 1930s: 'Put one or two stiff clothes-brushes in the men's cloakroom, so that they may repair between the dances the ravages caused by powder.'

Both authorities, however, agree on the nature of the food (a cold buffet, with champagne if possible); on the need for good musical arrangements (in the 1930s the cost of a band started at £5); on the etiquette of leave-taking (a discreet ceremony, lest the leave-takers break the party up; the Langley Moores even point out that the observances can in certain circumstances be omitted altogether); and on the floor. A polished floor, they point out, is best; a carpet-cloth of glazed canvas is a good substitute. Lady Colin adds a special plea against floor-waxing: 'A short time ago I was at a large ball in a county town where this was done, and the misery and vexation to which it gave rise were very great. Not only were our feet glued to the floor, to be severed only by a determined wrench at every step we took, but the destruction of dress was terrible.'

She also runs through the rules governing dancing partners: 'It is considered to be the duty of the son of the house to dance with each lady . . . . The number of times that a lady should dance with the same partner, except under special circumstances, should be limited . . . . When the music for the next dance begins, he conducts her to her chaperon.' These, by the Langley Moores' period, had become laughably obsolete, as had the chaperon herself.

The institution that both the rules and the chaperons had once regulated was, however, immortal. By the 1920s, certainly, a heavy programme of more informal activities had claimed the upper-class young. 'After a weary round of At Homes, *thés dansants*, private views and restaurant dinners, people ought to understand you can't always feel in the mood for footing it at their beastly dances,' runs the caption to a *Punch* cartoon of 1924; the pictures—five of them—show a dance in each case except the last, which features a bewildered hostess and a row of limp and languid *jeunesse*. But the Grand Dance, now staged for practical reasons in a hotel, had survived one world war comfortably and was all set to survive the next. (If this sounds a wildly obvious statement to make, it should be pointed out that no Victorian or Edwardian upholder of the social calendar could have conceived of the disappearance of that other key ingredient of social life, the formal call.) And another hardy perennial had survived with it: Presentation at Court would continue right through the inter-war period and on into the reign of Queen Elizabeth II.

Along with the great court balls (two in every Season, says the Countess of Lovelace, and 'very enjoyable'), presentation marked one of the highest peaks of an upper-class woman's career. The presence of the Sovereign—even of a tiny woman in black, who after an hour would hand over to her daughter-in-law, Alexandra—gave the event an aura that no upper-class entertainment, however glittering, could quite emulate. It was, in fact, usual for a lady to be presented both before and after marriage, but it is the before-marriage

occasion that is conjured up by those visions of trains and
white feathers. As solemn as any tribal ceremony of
initiation, presentation marked the moment when the
débutante—or beginner—could actually begin her journey
into Society.

As accounts show, that journey actually started at the foot
of the Throne itself. Here, outlined by social commentator
and satirist E. C. Grenville Murray, is how it felt to be
launched on that journey in 1881; his 'Flirt', to whose
adventures we will be returning frequently, would in modern
terms be dubbed a young girl in search of a husband.

She is taken to be presented at one of the Drawing rooms;
and if it be a novel delight it is also a trying one to find
herself driving down St James's Street with bare
shoulders in broad daylight. She sports a train three yards
long, and a pearl necklace. On descending from their
carriage in the palace-yard, she and her chaperon are
surrounded by young men in showy uniforms, military,
naval and diplomatic, who bustle to offer their arms and
murmur compliments. She is introduced to a youth in
blue swallowtail and kerseymere breeches—an *attaché*
home on leave—who begs to act as escort, and pilot her
through the crowded rooms, whilst a handsome young
giant in the scarlet-and-gold of the dragoons does the
same duty for the chaperon.
The press is so great and the scene so imposing that the
bashful girl is glad to accept the arm of the sucking-
diplomatist, who whispers to her the names of all the great
people whom they jostle. Here a past premier with his star
and garter; there a duchess and her daughter; there an
archbishop and his wife; droves of admirals pushing
nieces before them; and troops of generals doing their
best for flocks of damsels who were the belles of garrison-
towns. What a sight for a girl who has but just left the
schoolroom, and who, not a year before, received her last
whipping from a martinet governess!
The ceremony of curtsying to the Sovereign or the
Princess cheek-by-jowl with the greatest personages in the
land endows a girl with an assurance which never forsakes
her afterwards. She perceives that the great are not so
very formidable after all, and that good looks can hold
their own even at Court. From the circle of princes and

ministers grouped around the Throne, more than one admiring glance falls on her; and the Royal page who gathers up her train and chucks it over her arm as she retires from Royalty's presence does this more civilly than to titled dowagers with diamonds in their hair. Trust a girl, even a country-bred one, for noticing how many other girls, prettier than herself, there may be at one of these Drawing-rooms. The polite *attaché*, who joins her again after she has issued from the throne-room, mutters something nice about the grace with which she bears herself. He thinks her dress lovely, its train unique; and so forth.

The girl smiles; she only believes half those compliments (for she has had a first experience of flattery from country cousins at home), and yet she notices that guardsmen make way respectfully to let her pass; that grizzled veterans, whose breasts are covered with medals, nudge each other at her approach; and that sundry old ladies, with mortally plain daughters, eye her with that stony stare which, when it is levelled by woman at woman, is as good as purest incense. So, though her Majesty provides not so much as a cup of tea for the refreshment of her loyal subjects, who tire themselves in standing for hours in her saloons and other hours on the staircase waiting for their carriages, our incipient Flirt does not mind the fatigue. Her hair has got rumpled; her dress, disarranged in the crush, has lost half a yard of trimming; and one of her satin shoes is slipping off; but the *attaché* sticks close to her saying pleasant things, and the dragoon behind adds his word of testimony to the effect which her charms have produced. So this is to her a day of nectar-drinking. She has been presented at Court; she has had a success; and for that moment at least the world seems to be lying at her feet like a ball.

CHAPTER FIVE

~~~

Jeune fille à marier

'But, Mama, I don't want to marry him. I didn't know until it actually came to the point. I'd always meant to marry him, as you know. But, somehow, when he actually asked me . . . I just couldn't.'
'There, dear child, you musn't worry any more. You know perfectly well, don't you, that your father and I would not let you do anything you didn't want. It's a matter that only you can decide. After all, it's your life and your happiness at stake, not ours, isn't it, Ursula . . . but I *think* you'd better marry Edward.'

Evelyn Waugh,
Vile Bodies, 1930

Considered from a certain angle, presentation at court was not only the most glamorous event of the London Season but also the most democratic. The gauge for separating the 'suitable' entrants to Society from the 'unsuitable' was here set at its widest notch. There were, in all, only three qualifications for admittance to the throne room and, even taken together, the barrier they raised between Sovereign and subject (upper- or upper-middle-class subject) was not a high one.

The first was that the lady wishing to be presented should be of good moral and social character. The second, while seemingly more difficult to arrange, in practice presented few obstacles: presentation had to be made by someone who had already been presented. Obviously, the majority of débutantes and married women coming forward were daughters, nieces or more distant relatives of ladies who had been débutantes in their time, but the blood relationship was not essential. Anybody—as long as she herself had met the qualifications—would do, and, in view of the less than stringent nature of the rules, there was plenty of potential help around: help which did not, on occasion, shrink from demanding a large fee for services rendered.

The third qualification concerned the status of the actual presentee. The most obvious candidates, the daughters and wives of the aristocracy, had the privilege of themselves being kissed by Queen Victoria (no kisses were given or received if the Princess of Wales were acting as stand-in, and the practice was dropped altogether in the Edwardian period). Then came the ranks—the surprisingly large ranks—of those whose presentation would be sealed by the action of kissing the Queen's hand. They included the daughters and wives of the 'country gentry and town gentry', of the clergy, of naval and military officers, of professional men such as physicians and barristers, of merchants, bankers and members of the Stock Exchange and of 'persons engaged in commerce on a large scale'.

Court Drawing Rooms took place in the afternoon in Queen Victoria's time, during the evening in the reigns of her son and grandson. On the day appointed, the Victorian participants collected their courage, made a final un-dress practice of the complicated court curtsey and allowed themselves to be dressed in the costume demanded by regulation. Its essential features were a white silk dress with low bodice and very short sleeves, a train of velvet or satin at least three and a half yards long and a head-dress consisting of a white veil surmounted by the three Prince of Wales feathers. The Victorian deb's granddaughter, presented in 1934, would have worn very much the same: 'The King and Queen', wrote Janet Flanner, correspondent of the *New Yorker*,

> want gowns low and long, regardless of fashion; last year, stylish high-fronted numbers appeared. The King didn't like that. The Prince of Wales's three ostrich feathers, plus a twenty-seven-inch white veil, must be placed on the head in the *Ich Dien* motto manner; are an order, not an ornament; are often handed down from duchess to grandchild, the worse for wear. . . . The 1934 trains stretch eighteen inches back from the heel, are *manteaux de cour*, were four and a half yards long before the war, were cut off entirely in postwar 1919, and the following year cut down to the present two and a half yards from the shoulder.

(There was one major difference about the whole occasion, however: Grenville Murray's Flirt would have been pleased to find that the evening Drawing Rooms ended in supper, 'the King's catering being done by Lyons, the teashop people, and very good'.)

The train was the most difficult part of this finery to handle. Before the lovely moment when it was 'chucked over her arm', the débutante had first to keep her four yards of satin pristine and uncrushed in the ante-room crowds (once arrived at the Palace, it was very much a question of first come, first served). She then had to hope that the lords-in-waiting who spread it out for her in the throne room with ivory poles were poling it into the right place; and finally, and worst of all, she had to manoeuvre both herself and it out of the room backwards after making her curtseys. ('It wasn't really backwards, though—more of a sidle,' says one who remembers. 'And you *were* allowed to catch it up slightly.')

That was the worst moment; all that, in the Victorian period, was needed afterwards was patience and stamina. The double wait, before and after presentation, in a traffic jam of carriages, could last for hours, and there was a further queue to cope with at the court photographers' establishments. In Edward VII's time, things were speeded up. The telephone was used to summon a deb's transport, thus easing hold-ups; the buffet supper, served from tables laid with the Royal gold plate, helped to revive the wilting ladies; and some of the photographers took to serving a more modest collation themselves. Here, waiting their turn before the camera, the daughters of the nobility, the bishops and lesser clergy, the bankers, doctors and barristers gossipped and sipped coffee till dawn. They might all meet again at one of the State Balls or Drawing Rooms that they were now entitled to attend. But, as far as a true Top Society mamma could ensure, they would not spend over much time in each other's company elsewhere, still less with each other's families.

Even among those who had received the Sovereign's recognition, a rigid series of social barriers existed. In the 1890s, the newly-fledged Society hostess Elinor Glyn had it all explained to her: army and navy officers, she was told, could be invited to lunch or dinner, as could diplomats or clergymen. The local vicar might be a regular guest at Sunday lunch or supper, as long as he possessed the key qualification of being a gentleman. Doctors and solicitors were garden-party-only people; no lunch or dinner invitations could ever come their way. (The point about garden parties was that you did not introduce people to each other at them.) Elinor's instructor was Daisy, Countess of Warwick, her conversion to socialism well in the future and her awareness of Society rules still very much present. During the same bout of tuition she gave out-of-hand condemnation to anyone involved in commerce—but, as she ought to have known, the tide here was already turning. In the social set that had formed itself round the Prince of Wales (in whose affections she herself had supplanted Lily Langtry) the rich banker was not merely acceptable but welcomed.

The overall point, however, was that the two main divisions of 'gentleman's society'—the upper class proper and the upper-middles—should never in the purists' view be allowed to mix indiscriminately. And there were no greater purists in this connection than the mothers and chaperons handling the launch of a young girl into the marriage-market.

For marriage-market it was. Nobody in the pre-1914 era made any bones about the fact: marriage was a woman's sole career, and she owed it both to herself and to the family that had so far supported her to get on with it. Fundamentally, of course, this was an attitude that even the increase in opportunities for women between the wars did little to change: we have Jessica Mitford describing her mother's view (held in 1935) that 'the whole point of marriage was that it gave you something to do, a *façon d'être*, a house to run, a routine to follow; it provided the satisfying and constructive framework upon which a life and a future could be built.' And, at the present writer's guess, it is only within the last ten years that the idea of a woman having a work identity of equal, if not superior, value to her home identity has really gained general acceptance. But, for the overwhelming majority of girls emerging to play their part in the nineteenth-century social calendar, there was no question of achieving any work identity whatsoever. Florence Nightingale, Elizabeth Garrett Anderson, Sophia Jex-Blake were more than exceptions to the rule; to many of their contemporaries they were freaks who had totally de-classed and de-sexed themselves.

The ordinary young lady, and especially the Society young

lady, was as determined to make a good match for herself as a younger son of the period was to end up as a bishop or a general. In both cases, the motives were the same: status, allied to self-satisfaction, allied to the question of money. Where a girl was concerned, it was the duty of everyone—her mother, her mother's friends, her chaperon and her bill-settling father—to help her to achieve her ambition (it was also, one must not forget, their ambition too). She could not easily assess the prospects, trustworthiness and bank balances of potential suitors; they could. She, confronted with a dashing 'detrimental' or ineligible young man, might forget her overriding aim; they would remind her. (There was less to fear from two other ballroom types, the 'indefatigable' and the 'indispensable'. An indefatigable, according to a nineteenth-century débutante's diary, was 'either a young man just come out or an old beau who goes to three parties every evening, and dances indiscriminately with the old, the young, the pretty, the plain'. The indispensable was just what the term implied: an anxious fetcher and carrier of wraps, gloves, lemonade, fans, handkerchiefs and ices.) And if a débutante was by nature a giddy gad-about, both she and her parents were buttressed on all sides by the endless, minutely-detailed rules that social usage had evolved to control a business which was potential dynamite as far as class barriers were concerned: the choice of a permanent sexual partner.

That these regulations were all-pervading is indicated by the Countess of Lovelace, describing her Victorian girlhood.

Nearly every social custom which applied to ordinary intercourse between both sexes was based on the idea that every young woman, and especially every inexperienced girl, was a sacred thing to be carefully guarded from any possibility of insult or undue temptation. The well-guarded girl of the years 1870–80 could not walk alone in the street or drive alone in a cab or in a railway carriage. . . . How many a long dull summer afternoon have I passed immured indoors because there was no room for me in the family carriage and no lady's maid who had time to walk out with me. We lived near St James's Street and all the clubs, so that for my sisters or me to go out alone into the streets would have been to defy the social taboo in its severest form.

The taboo stemmed, she explains, from the notion (already not held with quite such vigour as formerly) that most men were capable of 'annoying—"or worse"—any unaccompanied young woman whom they met'. It was the 'or worse' factor that also accounted for the maze of regulations governing conduct on the dance-floor.

The young lady was not supposed to dance more than three dances with anyone. She was not supposed to sit a dance out. She was never supposed to vanish for any length of time at all; it was expected that she should be either on the arm of the young man who—under her chaperon's eye—had asked her to dance or sitting with the chaperon herself. Dance programmes (obsolete by the time Lady Colin Campbell revised her *Etiquette of Good Society*) regulated the thing still further. A quick glance at one of these would show any inquisitive parent exactly how things were shaping in her daughter's affairs, a particular indication being the dance immediately before supper: whoever secured that would be certain of the privilege of subsequently plying his partner with oyster patties, cold salmon, bonbons, champagne and tender conversation during the supper period itself.

As the Countess points out, the regulations were not always kept: 'the wise mother knew when to be negligent and when to enforce the rules.' (She adds that the need for 'going back to Mamma' was at times a welcome alibi.) Whatever the rule-book stipulated, girls and their favourite dancing-partners did sit dances out, did monopolise each other, did drift away to the balcony or lawn. But the basic framework of etiquette was such as to make the beginner's first dance an even more excruciating affair than it would be—and still can be—normally.

In the 1840s a Mrs Gore wrote a heart-rending account of this event for an essay collection called *Heads of the People*. Her heroine is an upper-middle-class deb called Adeliza Tibbs: eager, palpitating and hopeful of great things from her first ball. She is cursed, however, with a chaperon who cares more for food and whist than for her protégée's success.

On arriving at the dance, this jolly old gorgon plumps

herself down in the cardroom, and Miss Tibbs, of course, has to follow her. With a discreet amount of elbow-work, the débutante contrives to edge her chair forward so that the young men can at least see her through the ballroom doorway; her problem then is 'preserving the downcast air, insisted upon by her Chaperon as indispensable to the character of a Débutante, and keeping sufficiently on the alert to ascertain whether anything eligible in the way of partnership is approaching'.

Tucked away in the cardroom, she suffers appallingly. She knows that her one hope is to get on to the dance-floor, where she can display herself properly—but the only young man who actually notices her is scooped up by her hostess and led away to mingle elsewhere. Her chaperon then suggests supper.

Cramped with sitting three hours and a half upon a cane-bottomed chair, the Débutante is right glad to hook herself to the Chaperon's arm, elbow her way into the refreshment-room; and, while waiting half an hour for her turn to approach the table, and feeling the roses of her trimming crushed flat as crown pieces in the throng, she accepts the offer of some vanille [sic] ice, receives it over the head of a squat lady at the risk of dislodging it into her neighbour's turban or her own bosom; and, after soiling her gloves with a wet spoon, and getting her elbow jogged at every mouthful, to the imminent risk of her white satin slip, is anxious to crush her way back again into the dancing-room. The Chaperon, however, is still diligently at work on an overflowing plate of lobster salad, to which tongue and chicken, or a slice of galantine are likely to succeed. She has managed to obtain a snug berth for herself at the supper table; and is ensconced, with a glass of champagne at her right hand, a tumbler of sherry and water at her left, without any idea of giving in for twenty minutes to come.

At last the chaperon realises that things are not going well and has a whispered discussion with the hostess. Miss Tibbs shall dance at least once; there is, as it turns out, some urgency about the affair, since the carriage has been waiting for the last hour and her father is 'terribly particular' about his horses' well-being.

Five minutes afterwards, the lady brings up for judgment a genteel youth in nankeen pantaloons, an inch or two of whose meagre wrists are perceptible between the dress-coat he has outgrown and the overgrown gloves which wrinkle down over his thumbs; and whose straight, yellow hair is combed up, tent-wise, on the top of his head, like the brass flame with which the gas manufactories crown the ornamental bronze vases on their gate-posts; a shapeless booby, whose only care is not to giggle during the presentation. 'You *must* dance with him—it is her own nephew,' whispers the Chaperon, foreseeing the refusal of her charge; and with indignant soul, accordingly, poor Adeliza Tibbs deposits her fan and bouquet, and stands up, for the first time of her life, in the most insignificant corner of the most insignificant quadrille that has been danced in the course of the evening.

The first time, however, is also the worst time; as both Mrs Gore and Grenville Murray point out, and as all the hundreds of debs in the two commentators' respective periods and later were quickly to discover, the beginner soon gets the hang of things. 'A country Flirt', comments her biographer, 'has always to unlearn a great deal when she comes up to town.' But in no time she has unlearnt it sufficiently to be acquainted with 'nearly a couple of hundred unmarried men, whose names she cannot remember, and of whom she knows nothing more than that they have told her about themselves between the figures in a quadrille or during the panting halts of a waltz'. She becomes adept at distinguishing one London set from another; at speaking the off-hand slang of the ballroom; at accepting compliments without flickering an eyelash. More important still, she begins to learn how to connect faces with bank balances. Grenville Murray goes on to reconstruct a worldly (and financially embarrassed) mamma's advice to her daughter.

She bade her beware of £2,000 a year, which is but gilded misery; £5,000 with landed property, said she, was too often comparative pauperism, for the land ate up most of the income; £10,000 a year derivable from a bank or manufactory, and with an MPship annexed, would do as a *pis-aller*; but it would be foolishness not to pitch one's ambition on the best things at once, and go in straight for a coronet and £50,000 per annum. Such prizes, she told her, frequently fall to the lot of girls who have nothing but their good looks to bring their husbands.

(Notice the acceptability of 'trade' money; notice, too, that the writer was if anything *under*-estimating the amount of money a *bon parti* might bring to the contract. 'A century ago', says Roy Perrott in his analysis of the British aristocracy today, 'several lords had incomes of around £200,000 a year.') Before her first Season was out, the young lady stood an excellent chance of herself being able to 'price' her suitors down to the last farthing; it only remained to be seen whether she would act on such knowledge.

Just how far did families coax, pressurise or even strong-arm their daughters into marrying according to the dictates of the head rather than the heart? Taine, observing the scene in both the upper and upper-middle classes, felt that English girls enjoyed a freedom which ruled such methods out of court. 'A young English girl will not marry unless through inclination,' he says. 'Very often a lady, daughter of a marquis or baronet, having a dowry of £3000 or £3250, marries a simple gentleman, and descends of her own free will from a state of fortune, of comfort, of society, into a lower or much inferior grade.' What fortune-chasing went on, he continues, was entirely on the girl's—rather than the parents'—part: 'The reverse of the medal is the fishery for husbands. Worldly and vulgar characters do not fail in this respect; certain young girls use and abuse their freedom in order to settle themselves well. A young man, rich and noble, is much run after.' Azamat Batuk, observing the English social scene at much the same period, disagrees: 'In the present state of society,' he says revealingly, 'girls, besides being often married against their wish, are almost always quite unfit to understand what they are doing when they marry.'

It is probable that the truth usually lay somewhere between the two. Kindly parents would allow a girl to follow her inclination, as long as her suitor was, first, a gentleman and, second, one that could support her in reasonable style. The rigorous watchdog system under which she lived would, in any case, have allowed her to meet few who fell outside these well-defined limits. But a family that nourished ambitions of forging a link, through her, with either wealth or rank would be less likely to consider her feelings. Just one example—a transatlantic one; American mammas were by no means immune to class-consciousness, home-grown or practised on an international scale—is the case of the rich American eighteen-year-old Consuelo Vanderbilt. In the late 1890s, the ninth Duke of Marlborough (son of the anti-hero of the Blandford/Aylesford triangle) was wanting to restore Blenheim to its former glories. At the same time, Consuelo's mother was hoping to gain *entrée* to top English society. Consuelo was the intended link. She was brought over to meet the Duke, was unimpressed and on her return to the States fell in love with a fellow-American. Her mother—who later told a Vatican court that 'when I issued an order nobody discussed it. I therefore did not beg her but ordered her to marry the Duke'—went further than the well-known technique of emotional ('it'll kill me') blackmail; Consuelo became a prisoner in her own home. In the end, she accepted the man her mother had chosen for her. Her life as the Duchess of Marlborough started with tears on her wedding day and finally ended with divorce in 1921, following fifteen years' separation.

Parents might therefore bully, with lesser or greater prizes in mind. But they did not have it all their own way; the young ladies fought back. By the 1920s, of course, their freedom to do what they liked and kiss whom they liked was becoming fairly firmly established, at least amongst the most sophisticated (Waugh makes it clear that his unhappy Lady Ursula is old-fashioned by upbringing). 'The fashionable bridegroom', wrote Doris Langley Moore in 1929, 'does not insist upon virginity as a feature of his bride; he may even be a little disconcerted to find it.' (It is worth pointing out, however, that as late as the mid-30s a male house-party guest who preferred the privacy of his girl-friend's bedroom for some mild love-making incurred considerable displeasure: *he was not asked again.*) But, astonishing though it may seem, the girls of the high Victorian period also appear to have made discreet forays into unsupervised experiences of life and love.

The dashing elopments to the Continent or Gretna Green, the histories of love quietly triumphant in the Barrett Browning style, were only part of the story. The really clever girls were the ones who carried on a love life of almost modern intensity under the very noses of their guardians. That the young ladies could, in Victorian terms, 'fall' and get up again easily is explained with startling frankness by Grenville Murray: his 'garrison hack' (regimental flirt) starts with clandestine kisses and carries on from there. 'She thinks she can well defend herself, and so she does; until one day, her heart getting entangled within the wiles of an unusually good fellow, and champagne aiding, maybe, to throw her off her guard, her defences fail her at the wrong moment.' The garrison hack goes through a week of terrified dismay, then pulls herself together.

> The experienced maiden reflects that hidden faults are no faults, and that her aggressor is an honourable fellow who can keep a secret. He does keep it; and so do others subsequently, one after another, so fast as the careless Flirt treats them to fragments of her love. It is a maxim in such cases that what has been done once may be done again—that one may as well be hanged (if hanged at all) for twenty black sheep as for one white lamb: and the garrison hack's final consolation is that, 'They all do it!'

What is more, Grenville Murray points out, she still retains every chance of snaring a husband—a young and unknowledgeable one—and of making him an excellent wife.

Batuk, foreigner and visitor that he was, noticed something rather similar. His story is so odd, so circumstantial that it carries conviction: he fell victim to a young lady from the 'carriage-people' class who was, in modern terms, purely out for kicks.

His 'Miss Lucy' picked him up in Oxford Street, by using the positively antique method of dropping her purse. After a couple of not quite accidental meetings, she suggested that he take her and her sister to the Opera; then that they should meet in church; then that they should take a walk in the Park. After shelling out for the fans, handkerchiefs and opera tickets that Miss Lucy continually demanded, the scales finally fell from Batuk's eyes. But, at the cost of the £50 that he had been saving for his annual holiday, he decided to continue the association in a spirit of something like sociological enquiry.

He discovered that Miss Lucy was not, in fact, a courtesan; that her mother (no mention is made of a father) had no idea

Society tea-party: children
and dogs—both barred from
the drawing-room during
calling hours—are finally
admitted.

The parrot walk at London
Zoo.

Tightly packed guests at
London soirée, 1849.

The Victorian ball at its
most formal: the cream of
British and foreign Society
choose their partners at a
Buckingham Palace function.

1950: Mass curtsey by
débutantes at Queen
Charlotte's Ball.

Twentieth-century ballroom:
The Chelsea Arts Ball, here
photographed in the 1950s,
had provided Society with
one of its earliest successful
introductions to
unconventional behaviour.

1887: meeting Her Majesty
at a Buckingham Palace
garden party.

Hyde Park regulars wait to
catch a glimpse of the
Princess of Wales' carriage.

Presentation queue:
débutantes of 1895 get ready
to enter the Royal presence.

The simplified dinner table
of the 1930s: even the
buffet spread in the
background seems thin in
comparison with the lavish
lay-outs of the Edwardian
period.

For the ladies, high fashion;
for the seamstress, 'sheer
bravura display'.

(*Above from left to right*)
Preserving their superiority:
(i) in the Edwardian period.
(ii) in 1910.
(iii) after the First World
War.
(iv) in the 1930s.

(*left*) 1910's 'Black Ascot':
Society racegoers in
mourning for Edward VII.
Note the correct way of
holding up a skirt.

(*Right*) Fashions in holidays:
the spa.

Fashions in holidays: the sun-deck.

British Society—in this case, British
residents in Pekin—carries on as
usual: the scene is the British
Legation, soon to be besieged in the
Boxer Rising.

Tea in Bangalore: servants
outnumber eaters by three to one.

A culture transplanted: the Ootacamund Hunt and guests meet for a hunt breakfast at the hill station's Club.

Accessory to the fact.

Parasols at Ascot . . .

. . . and umbrellas.

Boundary shot at the Eton
and Harrow match.

1892: Henley Regatta by
day (*above*) and by night.

Yachting at its most
aristocratic. The Prince of
Wales, soon to be Edward
VII, is on the far left, while
his wife Alexandra, leans on
a chair, centre.

Cowes, 1930: steerswoman
and passenger.

Riding in Hyde Park's
Rotten Row.

English scene in November.

(*Opposite above*) Heading
towards freedom: but
inflatable tyres will bring
freedom considerably
nearer.

(*Opposite below*) Country
house: croquet in the
mid-nineteenth century.

1958, and Hungarian Ullein Revilsky makes history; she was the last débutante to be presented at Buckingham Palace.

But thousands continue to attend Palace garden parties.

of what she was up to; that her main accomplice in her escapades—which included dinner in a private restaurant room, an unthinkable thing for a young lady—was the family coachman, who demanded a fine line in tips from her escorts; and that other foreigners in London had met similar girls, 'your Misses Lucy apparently being of the opinion that we are more *sans gêne* than you, have no chance of compromising them, as we are today in London and to-morrow in Spain or Turkey, and, above all, present some attraction of novelty.'

He also noted a remarkable snatch of conversation:

I remember, for instance, asking her once what she generally does, and how she spends her time when neither shopping nor visiting. 'I sing, I play,' answered she; 'sometimes I paint a little. Then I read, of course. What should I do? What everybody does . . . . When tired of all that, I cry.'

'You cry?—why?' asked I, quite astonished by this unexpected avowal.

'Because I like to cry. I sometimes feel so utterly miserable and dull. Crying always does me good in such moments.'

Batuk's article on Miss Lucy brought him into considerable public censure. He was vindicated, however, when a piece from another source appeared carrying the statement: 'If we may credit the communications which, within the last six months, have been addressed to us, there are far too many London girls living with wealthy and respectable parents who act as Miss Lucy did, and many more who would desire to do so.' This, Batuk commented, gave a hint of the 'existence of something worse than what I supposed'.

But even the most skilful of Miss Lucys would probably end up one day at the altar. Leaving aside considerations of love and even money, marriage was, indeed, their only permanent refuge from a reputation that suddenly threatened to change from mere sportiness into something much worse. For more respectable girls, though, the announcement of an engagement was something to be welcomed with joy unmixed with shuddering relief. Short of death or disaster, they were now set on the only road to self-fulfilment: fulfilment through their children, through the management of an establishment, through the exercise of social skills, through the intoxicating social power they

had seen their mothers and, even more important, their
grandmothers wield in the afternoon drawing-rooms.
Presentation at court was just a start: a girl's real transition
from Nobody to Somebody came now. From the moment of
her marriage, she could enter the stage of the national social
calendar as a fully paid-up member of the club that had
constructed it.

What, from her point of view, made this glorious future all
the more certain was that her fiancé, having declared himself
to her parents, was now honourably bound to go through
with the marriage unless she herself released him. 'It is
always recognised, of course, that the actual severance of the
tie must come from the girl,' says a turn-of-the-century
Etiquette of Marriage. 'So much is necessary whether she be
the defaulter or no, for no girl should be put in the position
of being given up or "jilted" as unkind friends would be sure
to term it.'

The anonymous author goes on to point out that no girl 'of
spirit or sense' would keep a man to his bargain against his
will; all the same, the girl's power, from being negligible, has
suddenly become enormous. 'In contrary cases, a girl can
always more easily claim her freedom. No blame is imputed
to her for changing her mind, but the unfortunate swain who
is in such a predicament is usually harshly spoken of by
society. This is scarcely fair.'

Fair or not, it was the system. Also part of the system was
the orgy of preparation, very similar to that of today, that
followed the announcement that a marriage had been
arranged. Indeed, it was in most particulars the *same* as that
of today. No section of the regulations governing the social
moves of the Top Victorians has survived quite so well, so
untouched by war, by the emancipation of women and by the
redistribution of wealth as the business of getting married.

'The wear and tear of mind is indescribable, more
particularly to the members of the bride-elect's family,' said
Lady Colin Campbell, her comments applying to past,
present and future alike.

The trousseau—whom to ask to be bridesmaids—the
guests to be invited to the wedding and to the wedding-
feast—who ought to be invited to stay in the house during
the time—how to provide for visitors who cannot be
so accommodated—the perplexing question whether

hospitality is to take the form of breakfast, luncheon, or afternoon tea—the amusement of the guests for the rest of the day—these and all the thousand and one details consequent on them are no light burden to support.

In the Edwardian period, the fashionable time for weddings was 2.30, although in the nineteenth century it had to be much earlier. (The legally recognised time then for the celebration of marriage was between eight in the morning and noon.) In the bride's home the hours immediately before the event would be spent anxiously overseeing the preparations for food (cold game, cold ham, savoury jellies, custards, candied fruits, the Cake, claret, champagne and coffee), in controlling and marshalling the house-party and—in the bride's case—in putting on a uniform of purity that in many ways resembled her presentation dress of a short while before. In the mid-nineteenth century, it would in fact have been something approximating to evening dress, displaying arms and neck to advantage; by the Edwardian era, bridal gear was simpler and more modest, while the groom had forsaken an evening suit of the type his father had worn for the occasion in favour of morning dress.

At the appointed minute, the pair embarked on the process that celebrated their becoming man and wife: the bride's procession up the aisle on her father's arm; the stately progress to the vestry (where the best man discreetly settled the ceremony's fees); the drive home; the wedding breakfast, with the bride's mother on the bridegroom's right and the father of the bride on the bride's left; the cutting of the cake; and the departure of the couple, now in travelling costume, followed by showers of rice and old shoes. Then followed the let-down moment when no one, suddenly, had anything to do.

Guests not staying at the house were expected to leave as soon as they could, while the older members of the house-party needed no persuasion to vanish for a spell in their rooms; it was the younger ones who presented the problem. Lady Colin had the answer: 'The wisest thing to do is to send all the young people for a drive.' And, obviously, this course allowed the unmarried female section of the party to continue to bring all their attention, wit and accomplishments to furthering themselves in the one and only career that they were allowed to understand.

CHAPTER SIX

∾∾∾

Religion

Well, Little D., after all it *is* the Church of England, we
have to support it, don't you see?
> Lady Redesdale, recalled and reported by
> Jessica Mitford,
> *Hons and Rebels,* 1960

The overwhelming majority of Top Victorians and
Edwardians got married in church. It was in church, too, that
they made their first public appearance: squirming,
red-faced bundles of Honiton lace, clutched first by their
nervous godmothers and then, the baptism safely over, by
their nurses. It was in church that their equals would
formally mark and mourn their death.

So far, the pattern is one that is still copied today; but,
unlike today, church-going occupied a far more important
place in the nineteenth-century social calendar than that. As
the Countess of Lovelace says, on each and every Sunday in
London, 'the great majority of us went as a matter of course';
it was as a matter of course, too, that they would attend
Sunday morning service in the country.

Not, it should be noted, evening service; Evensong, in
London at least, was what the servants went to. And this was
not the only social distinction that was allowed to creep into
the business; in fact, the whole question of religious
observance was as riddled by the rules of the upper-class
game as the most formal of balls. At a ball, or driving in the
Park, members of Society were expressing solidarity with
their class; in church, they were expressing solidarity with
God. 'It was, they felt, only right and proper to pay their
tribute to the Almighty for his wisdom in creating them,'
comments Percy Colson with only mild sarcasm, 'and to
thank Him for His unfailing patronage of the nobility and
gentry.' Adding that Society in the Season had its own
especially favoured churches, he points out that a visit to St
George's, Hanover Square, St Paul's, Knightsbridge, Holy

Trinity, Sloane Street, or St Peter's, Eaton Square, was like 'going to a religious party, so numerous were the carriages driving the fashionable world to worship'.

But it was less the choice of church than the choice of Church that presented the upper and upper-middle classes with their principal way of marking themselves off on Sundays from the general public; indeed, with one of their principal methods of doing so on any day of the week. The British Christian of our period had three paths open to him: Roman Catholicism (Roman Catholics had been given the right to sit in Parliament in 1829); Anglicanism; and the conglomerate of Nonconformist sects that can conveniently be brought together under the heading of 'Chapel'. Of these, the Roman Catholics presented a special case, as will be seen later. Of the two Protestant churches, Chapel almost by definition found its congregations among those who did *not* belong to Society or to upper-middle-class society. 'Methodism, for example, grew up partly to give its adherents a "society" of their own,' says one expert. 'One of its benefits was that it gave a sense of community to people who otherwise did not have one.' Indeed, it can be argued that the misty lowest reaches of 'gentility' stopped where the upper sector of Chapel society started; this, in the instance of a South Coast town in the 1930s, included the local butcher, the harbourmaster, the one and only stationer in town, several teachers, two small farmers and the local solicitor's managing clerk. The solicitor himself, of course, worshipped in church.

There remained Anglicanism in its various forms, and it was to this that the Top Victorians and their successors gave their allegiance—not out of any conscious spirit of choice but simply because they thought it fitting. Why they thought it fitting is explained in all its subtlety by Taine, who found that the English mind, with its firm belief in the 'moral being', was a natural breeding-ground for religious susceptibility of a certain type.

'The Church of England', he says,

has on her side antiquity, her alliance with the State, her privileges, her endowments, her bishops seated in the House of Lords, her preponderance in the Universities, her mean position between the two extremes, between the faith, the dogma, and the spirit of the Puritans, and the faith, the dogma, and the spirit of the Roman Catholics. In the first place, she is an old and legal compromise, and this suits the majority, which everywhere loves compromises, willingly follows tradition, and is obedient to the law. Moreover, she is rich, she is a power in the State, she has ties among the aristocracy, she has good connections, she is one of the organs of the Constitution, and, in virtue of all these titles, she finds favour among statesmen, among Conservatives, among men of the world, among all those who wish to be considered 'respectable' . . . .

To crown all, her Prayer-Book is very beautiful, her services are noble and impressive, her conduct is semitolerant, she permits some play to the free judgment of the individual. Thus accredited, she proposes and imposes her version, and it may be said that this version is generally accepted.

The country landowner, dozing in his box-pew with his family and guests beside him, might have boggled faintly at this if confronted with it all of a lump; if, however, he had gone through it point by point, he would have nodded approval at each one. Old, legal, well-connected; moderate in its approach and demands, noble and impressive in its manifestations; headed by no less a person than the Sovereign; and extremely rich—the Church of England was yet another facet of what we today call the Establishment and of what its Top Victorian members would just have seen as the proper scheme of things.

This feeling of a neatly-ordered pattern was reinforced by the glimpse that the landowner had had of his church before closing his pew-door on the view (in many cases, he could think of it as 'his'; where the living was in his gift, he had the right to choose the officiating clergyman). There, spread out behind him, were all his fellow-worshippers, publicly arranged for their spiritual business according to their temporal estate.

In *Lark Rise to Candleford*, Flora Thompson recalls the order that prevailed in the church of the Lark Rise 'mother village', with its congregation of thirty: 'the farmer's family in the front row, then the Squire's gardener and coachman, the schoolmistress, the maidservants, and the cottagers, with the Parish Clerk at the back to keep order'. (It would have been unusual for the Squire's personal employees not to have been C of E themselves; in addition, the period at this point was not long past when the cottagers' only hopes of getting a village schooling for their children lay in their Church of England membership.) The clergyman's family had a pew opposite the Squire's in the chancel; the clergyman's daughter played the harmonium. Here, as at all the other 'Broad Church' churches in England, the service would have unfolded according to the middle-of-the-road Anglican tradition: the psalms, Hymns Ancient & Modern and a sermon on a moral rather than a theological subject. A favourite topic, as Laura of Lark Rise noticed, was 'the supreme rightness of the social order as it then existed'.

That this Establishment idyll was not totally uniform was quite clear even to foreign visitors like Taine, who distinguished two further variants. 'One, which is the more aristocratic, leans more upon authority, has the greater fondness for ritual, is called the High Church; the other, which is more popular, more ardent, more eager to make conversions and renovate the heart, is called the Low Church party.' The few Evangelicals in Society—Lord Shaftesbury was one—worked not so much to protect the established social order as to soften the harsher effects its distinctions produced; the concern of the High Church members, on the other hand, was almost entirely with the soul. Neither movement held much attraction for the 'rich man in his castle' type of churchgoer who could quite happily recite the Athanasian Creed and, like the Duke of Sussex of an earlier period, not believe a word of it.

Many members of the High Church's most enthusiastic group, the Oxford Movement, ended—as their shocked contemporaries would have said—by 'going over to Rome'. The average Church of England member had a horror of 'Rome' that was only minimally doctrinal. Rome was foreign; Rome was emotional in its appeal; Rome, as the sub-literature of the time never tired of pointing out, was the inspiration of the Inquisition, Bloody Mary and the practice of walling up nuns alive. 'If you want a novel to hot you up against the Catholics, I've got the most shocking one here,' says Gwen Raverat's Aunt Etty in *Period Piece*. The aunt, one of the many notable figures in Mrs Raverat's Cambridge childhood, had hit on a harrowing account of a priest who rode so fast to give a dying man absolution that he killed his horse under him; 'isn't it *horrible*!'

These prejudices, though, did not touch those Catholics who formed part of the Upper Ten Thousand. At least one Roman Catholic priest—Father Bernard Vaughan, who preached at Farm Street on the sins of Society—became the darling of that same Society and was frequently invited to country houses. All the same, the great Catholic families formed a very special set within the whole, and for an obvious reason. A Society family had among its aims the ambition of securing suitable and profitable marriages for all its members. But it would not count it profit to see its line changed forever into a Roman Catholic one. 'Once a C of E duke, always a C of E duke,' was the general motto. This, while keeping them closely knit as a group, presented the Roman Catholics themselves with difficulties; as, on his heroine's behalf, Evelyn Waugh points out in *Brideshead Revisited*, 'there could be no eldest son for her, and younger sons were indelicate things, necessary, but not to be much spoken of.'

His Lady Julia, a Roman Catholic deb of the 1920s, goes on to brood on the alternatives, which were not at all encouraging.

> There were, of course, the Catholics themselves, but these came seldom into the little world Julia had made for herself; those who did were her mother's kinsmen, who, to her, seemed grim and eccentric. Of the dozen or so rich and noble Catholic families, none at that time had an heir of the right age. Foreigners—there were many among her mother's family—were tricky about money, odd in their ways, and a sure mark of failure in the English girl who wed them. What was there left?

The Catholic members of the upper classes were at least long-pedigreed Britons and Christians both; another group of candidates for upper-class acceptance had a semantic claim only on the first qualification and none at all on the second. They were the Jews. That mid-Victorian Britain viewed even its most high-ranking and cultivated Jewish citizens with profound suspicion is shown by the political career of Baron Lionel de Rothschild: from 1847 onwards, the electors of the City of London repeatedly chose him as their Member of Parliament, and yet he was not allowed to take his seat at Westminster. The obstacle was the Parliamentary Oath, which contained the words 'on the true faith of a Christian'. Only after eleven years of controversy was this phrase made an optional one and non-Christians thereby permitted to become functioning MPs.

A prominent leader on the side of reform here was Benjamin Disraeli; among the opposition, and demonstrating the strictly selective nature of his reforming impulses, was Lord Ashley, later to be Lord Shaftesbury. The Jews, Lord Ashley held, were 'voluntary strangers here, and have no claim to become citizens but by conforming to our moral law, which is the Gospel'. Another opponent preached the crucial importance of ensuring that anyone who had a hand in the country's government should be a member of the country's accepted religion. On this score, Disraeli's own presence in the House was due to his father, who in the early nineteenth century had grown increasingly disaffected with synagogue affairs and had finally had the teenage Benjamin received into the Church of England.

In 1874, Disraeli had, in his own words, reached the 'top of the greasy pole'. Before him were six years as Prime Minister, a peerage and death one year after quitting office. In that time, he would also enjoy the wholehearted support and friendship of Queen Victoria. But, amongst the conservative courtiers who made up the Queen's own circle, he won no such support or liking for members of his race in general. The Queen was charmed by his suggestion that she should take the title of Empress of India; the elder stateswomen of Society were anything but pleased at the prospect of receiving his friends the Rothschilds—whose money had, incidentally, secured the Suez Canal for the British.

However, Queen Victoria's son did what the Queen herself had not seen fit to do. She would admit only Disraeli into her friendship; the Prince of Wales, to her illogical horror, welcomed the Rothschilds and other millionaires such as David Sassoon and Baron Hirsch. Hirsch, in fact, became the Prince's unofficial financial adviser; when the Queen refused to invite him to a Buckingham Palace concert, the Prince took it as a personal slight.

By the end of the nineteenth century, a new social grouping in the upper classes had become firmly established. Individual members of Society had to choose whether to ally themselves with the old ironclads or with the rich, jolly, high-living and—in the ironclads' view—*fast* men and women that clustered round the Heir Apparent. A handy name for them is the 'pre-Edwardians'. That Society's traditional source of ready cash, its land, was becoming increasingly unreliable only served to make the choice between the two sets more imperative: in the Prince's group it did not matter what your religion, your source of income, your nationality or (within the limits of discretion) your morals were, as long as you could obey the set's rules. Its aims were frankly materialistic: reacting against the crushing rigours of true Victorian etiquette, the pre-Edwardians had plenty of time in which to develop the free-spending style of life that would later be associated with their leader's reign. When, in 1901, he came to the throne, the Victorian concepts of who was or was not acceptable vanished in a flood of champagne, cream and turtle soup.

Three years later, an anonymous foreign observer in London commented that the only source of 'humanising influences' in the fashionable world were its Jewish members. It is ironic that this much-needed element should have been provided by a group that Society had, in the main, been battling for years to keep out.

Church Parade, 1892

CHAPTER SEVEN

∽∽∽

Food

Partridges à la Victoria: A remove dish will require three or four birds. The partridges must be partially boned, by removing the whole of the breast-bone from the interior, without in any degree deforming the breast. The birds must be reasonably filled with game forcemeat in which there have been mixed a few truffles cut in small dice, and are to be trussed up round and plump, and being closely and neatly larded, should be braised in wine mirepoix (recipe no. 300). When the partridges are done, their stock must be strained, freed from all grease, and used for making some brown sauce, to which, after it has boiled, been skimmed, and properly finished, add a small pat of anchovy butter, or a very little essence, half a glass of sherry, and a tiny pinch of cayenne; and use this sauce to pour over the partridges when dished up; furnish round with mushrooms au gratin, and serve.'
C. E. Francatelli, chief cook to HM The Queen,
The Cook's Guide & Butler's Assistant, 1880

'How strange', muses the hero of *The Edwardians*, a young and introspective duke, 'that eating should play so important a part in social life.' Strange, maybe, but a practice so time-honoured as to appear inevitable. By the time that Edward, Prince of Wales, came into his own, his upper- and upper-middle-class subjects were set on an annual collision course with raging dyspepsia. The dish that Miss Sackville-West has set before her young duke's fellow-diners is, for example, a quintessentially Edwardian invention of *pâté de foie gras*, inside a truffle, inside an ortolan, inside a quail.

Doing oneself really well was, of course, no new thing to the richer members of British society, who through the centuries had provided foreigners and indigenous satirists with a panoramic spectacle of red-faced, pop-eyed, beer-swilling meat-eaters. Wine was good for you too.

75

Princess Charlotte, daughter of George IV and heir to the British throne, was thought (mistakenly) to have died in childbirth because of the starvation diet she had been prescribed: it had lacked red meat, red wine and general heartiness. Her death was the first in the chain of events that brought Alexandrina Victoria into existence (her father had been quite happily living with his French mistress for fifteen years until Parliament told him to find a marriageable princess at once) and on to the throne.

During Victoria's sixty-three-year reign, however, three major changes overtook the business of Top People's eating; we are still, when not hunched over our telly-trays, living with the results. The first was a change in the time of the main meal of the day. Dinner, the gathering-point of the whole family, was as late as the eighteenth century eaten in the early afternoon; in the nineteenth it shifted to the evening and, if eaten on a really lavish scale, took up much of it. Supper—once the other main gathering—was pushed almost off the daily calendar of events altogether and took a subsidiary place in the timetables of those who dined during the day, of those who had been out late or of those who were giving a dance. Breakfast remained where it was; but there was now an aching void where dinner had been. It was, of course, filled by lunch: nursery lunch for the children, lunch at the club for male refugees from the rigours of the social round (if they belonged to the Reform, the great Francatelli himself would have inspired much of what they ate), an elegant bite for the ladies. It was the ladies themselves who added tea; or, rather, afternoon tea. Another sort of tea—with hot muffins, crumpets, toast, cold salmon, pies, ham, roast beef, fruit in season, cream and both tea and coffee—found its own way into the more active and informal programme of the country house.

The second change also concerned dinner. From the time of the Normans to the middle of the nineteenth century, a dinner-table in British polite society looked rather like a dinner-table in an Indian restaurant today. A whole course would be put on the table at once, and a course consisted of not one dish but many. The diners of the Middle Ages did themselves particularly proud, with twelve or so dishes to each course of a coronation feast in 1399. People dipped, tasted and gourmandised as they chose; then the remains were taken away and another 'course' brought on. The coronation feast referred to—it celebrated the crowning of Henry IV—had three vast courses, each of which ended with a 'subtlety' or fancy model made out of sugar and marzipan; by the nineteenth century, both courses and dishes were slightly fewer in number. Even so, a first course might well consist of soup, salmon, roast lamb, fowl with rice, fillets of beef, more fowl (in croquettes) and pigeons. And diners still picked and chose from the spread before them, asking dinner-table neighbours or servants to pass the veal cutlets from their station further up the table. As the nineteenth century progressed, though, this system of bawling out for the roast quails was increasingly felt to be less than elegant, and service à la Russe was introduced. A la Russe meant, quite simply, that each individual dish was served from a side table; when finished with, it was taken away and replaced by another, thus becoming a 'course' in its own right.

Despite the grumblings of diehards, a more fragmented pattern was quickly established of soup (possibly with a choice), fish (also possibly with a choice), entrées and removes (definitely with choices; they formed the main meat courses), game, sweets, ices and fruits.

The third change, again, had its principal effect on dinner, although there was a backwash to lunch and even to breakfast. In the industrial age, comments the biographer of the British eater, Philippa Pullar, to be rich and successful 'was your God and your country's reward for services. Your worldly possessions not only pointed to your abilities in the Roman way—but also they pointed out how *good* you were.'

She goes on: 'The nineteenth century shows a great rise in entertaining. The houses and dining rooms were stages on which to display abilities and possessions. Dinner parties were convenient means of showing to friends, neighbours and competitors, the china, pretty wife and quantity of food one could afford.' She does not mention servants; labour, in the nineteenth century, was extremely cheap. But a second glance at the quotation at the head of this chapter will show what even a middle-class kitchen (the book is expressly aimed at the middle classes) was expected to come up with in terms of both raw materials and personnel.

A hostess-cook-housekeeper of the 1970s will immediately notice the danger-spots in Francatelli's recipe. The cooking of the partridges is simplicity itself; even boning the beastly

little things is merely a matter of practice. What makes the
whole dish so complicated is the number of 'dishes within
dishes' that it calls for. There are five in all: the game
forcemeat, the mirepoix, the sauce, the anchovy butter and
the mushrooms. Recipe 300 is no joke in itself: 'take red
carrots, onions, celery, parsley-roots, shallots, raw ham or
bacon, cloves, mace and peppercorns' . . . .' Nor yet is the
degreasing of the stock a particularly easy job. And this
would be only *one* dish among many, designed to take its
place, say, alongside capon *à la piemontaise*, chicken *à la
romaine* or roast sirloin of beef. No one, obviously, was
expected to eat their way through every item on a Victorian
menu, and many people would have tasted less than half the
dishes they were offered; but, given a basis of this sort, the
culinary part of Britain's social calendar needed few
embellishments to prepare it for the period when the
country's most noted *bon viveur* was also its King.

Of all the attributes of the Edwardian era, its legendary
breakfasts are, along with its chorus girls, possibly the most
famous. The silver chafing dishes and the smell of coffee; the
hot rolls, muffins and toast; the fruit; the devilled kidneys,
kedgeree, eggs, broiled trout, bacon; the porridge; the game
pie, galantine, tongue, cold grouse, cold ham and
obsessively-relished ptarmigan . . . the picture evoked is
ravishing or repulsive, according to fancy. What everyone
agrees on is how incredible these breakfasts were
gastronomically. In extent they certainly were (although,
again, you picked and chose), but not in content. The
full-scale British breakfast, as served in the 1970s by British
Rail, also has its fruit element (orange juice), its cereals, its
bacon, eggs, mushrooms and preserved meats (sausages); its
optional fish; and its rolls or toast. And this writer
remembers being presented with an 8 am spread in a
Norwegian youth hostel that went easy on the hot dishes but
threw in cold meat, cold herring, cold apple stew and cheese
for good measure.

The Edwardian breakfast was an informal, serve-yourself
meal, as was lunch. Servants might be present at a large
luncheon to bring in the soup and hand the hot or cold first
courses (cold fowls, cold lamb, cold pigeon, cold pie and
ptarmigan again); they would then leave the eaters to deal
with the puddings, jellies, cheese, biscuits and fruit by
themselves, happily creating what Lady Colin Campbell calls

an 'elegant disorder' on the table. Dinner, however, was entirely different. A successful dinner party was not only a demonstration of your wealth, your cook's skill and your elegant taste in home-making; for a Victorian or Edwardian hostess it represented a pinnacle of social achievement. So very much more went into it than mere cooking.

Assuming that she had ample kitchen staff and the right quantity and quality of table furniture—a party of twelve would call for, among other things, forty-eight forks, six sauce ladles, asparagus tongs, twenty-four sherry glasses, six carafes, twenty-four dinner napkins, twelve fish napkins and a spotless white damask tablecloth—a lady would set about giving a dinner party in the following manner. First, a month or more before the party took place, she would consider her guest list. It would be composed mainly of married couples, with a few unmarrieds to add youth and/or interest. They would not necessarily all know each other, but they would be of much the same social standing. (For a reason that will become clear, a guest list composed of people of *exactly* the same social standing would be an invitation to disaster.) In addition, she would make sure she had a quota of good talkers, good listeners and good mixers. The invitations would go out and be answered within twenty-four hours.

Nearer the date, the hostess would review both the menu and her servants (the wines were the traditional province of the host). It was considered more correct that the guests should be waited on by male staff rather than by women, a consideration that the hostess would have taken into account when deciding the numbers for her party; but if, by some unforeseen catastrophe, a gap in the serving ranks appeared, she had two options. One was to press one of the outdoor male staff to her aid; the other was to use one of the resident female domestics. Since speed, dexterity and quietness were the essential qualifications for the job, the maid was usually the better choice.

On the day itself, the house would go into action. The tableware would be polished, the table itself laid and adorned with silver candlesticks, individual menu-cards, flowers and quantities of maidenhair fern. In the lower regions of the house, the scene would be one of organised turmoil. The hostess herself would brood over her seating-plan—name-cards on the table would show where each diner was to sit—and re-check another social calculation. The way from the drawing-room to the dining-room would be led by her husband, and on his arm would be the most important, most aristocratic or oldest female guest present. The others would follow according to the ladies' ranking-order, and the hostess would bring up the rear on the arm of the most important male guest.

Once assembled (lack of punctuality would cover the latecomer in tingling embarrassment), the party would get down to business very rapidly. Pre-dinner drinks were not served; after a maximum of twenty minutes in the drawing-room, the guests would be trooping in to their meal, which started sometime between 8 and 9. The ladies would pull off their gloves; soup would be set before each guest who, as etiquette allowed, started straight in without waiting; and the long, lavish parade of food got under way. No one would be so bumpkinish as to take a second helping of anything; conversely, no one would be burdened by officious urgings to taste the sweetbreads once these had been refused. Non-drinkers would be offered mineral water.

The final stage came when the dessert, finger bowls and wine were placed on the table (until this point, wine had been dispensed by the butler) and the servants withdrew. Soon, the hostess would 'collect eyes'; the party would stand, the man nearest the door opened it, and the ladies swept out. Their coffee was served in the drawing-room. The men would have theirs—along with their port, nuts and cigars—still sitting round the dining-table. The hard drinking of the eighteenth and early nineteenth centuries being no longer acceptable, the male guests would join their women-folk within twenty minutes or so, after which the party drank tea, collected itself and left. By 11.30, the evening was over.

And so, in 1914, was the whole feast. The war's effect on the social pastime of eating, as on every single aspect of the social calendar, was drastic. Men—guests and servants alike—were at the front or convalescent or dead; women were frequently in mourning or munition factories or both. Restaurants, which had been steadily growing in number during the 1900s and now included renowned establishments such as the Trocadero, the Criterion and the dining-rooms of the great hotels, were in 1916 ordered to serve no more than three courses between 6 and 9.30 pm and no more than two courses at any other time. Rationing was introduced. 'In most chic restaurants of the West End,' Arnold Bennett wrote in the war's penultimate year, 'you cannot get butter, or any substitute for it, at either lunch or dinner.' What a soldier on his brief leaves from the front wanted in the way of entertainment was a theatre review and a drink; night-clubs provided this when pubs, hampered by licensing hours, could not.

That this total dislocation of four years changed the attitudes of the rich Briton to food is shown by a single sentence from *The Pleasure of Your Company*. 'The one unpardonable fault in entertaining,' the Langley Moores wrote in the 1930s, 'is pretentiousness.' The point is made still further by a menu that they suggest for a dinner party. This runs:

Iced Melon

Lentil Cream Soup

Grilled salmon trout   Sauce tartare
(or other grilled fish in season)

Roast Chicken

Potato Rissoles   Aubergines

Asparagus   Sauce Hollandaise

Banana splits   Vanilla cream

Cheese Ramequins

Dessert

The meal would be accompanied by wine (although not, as before the war, by a different wine for every dish) and preceded by sherry or cocktails. But, hostesses are warned, 'extravagant and fantastic cocktails are no longer in the height of fashion.'

The cooking and serving of a dinner such as this would certainly require domestic help; today, a meal on such a scale would be feasible only if undertaken by a hotel or a firm of commercial caterers. But, with the possible exception of the savoury, it still is undertaken on any occasion when a medium-grand dinner is required. A modern do-it-yourself hostess would leave out either melon or soup, either fish or

meat and the ramequins and serve something that taxed
neither her expertise nor her guests' sense of what was
fitting. The patterns laid down by Francatelli and his
contemporaries and brought to a final point of luscious
perfection in the first decade of this century still persist, even
if in a less elaborate form. But there can be few people now
who have ever tasted ptarmigan; let alone at breakfast.

'Theatre Blouses', 1898

CHAPTER EIGHT

∽∾∽

Clothes

There is no time, sir, at which ties do not matter.
P. G. Wodehouse,
Jeeves and the Impending Doom,
The Jeeves Omnibus, 1931

If, to a large extent, the day-to-day social calendar was founded on the consumption of food, clothes gave it its main means of adornment. And not adornment alone: clothes proclaimed both the man and the gentleman—and the gentlewoman. They provided, and still provide, one of the key methods of identification that allowed members of the British upper classes to spot their equals.

Working from next the skin outwards, let us watch two women of the twentieth century getting ready for a party. The first, described by Miss Sackville-West, is an Edwardian duchess, mother of the young duke mentioned in the last chapter. She is middle-aged, fashionable and very rich. The second—also rich, also middle-aged, also fashionable and observed in her bedroom by a real-life contemporary—belongs to the 1930s.

Edwardian Lucy (nothing to do with Batuk's Miss Lucy, who belongs to a different period and milieu altogether) starts her toilette by having her hair done. Under a barrage of scolding, her maid Button brushes it, curls it on heated tongs, back-combs it and piles it over 'rats' or hair-pads. These were, the author comments, 'unappetising objects, like last year's birds'-nests'. The duchess then vanishes into her dressing-room and embarks on an operation correctly visualised by her daughter waiting outside.

Viola knew well enough what was going on: her mother was seated, poking at her hair meanwhile with fretful but experienced fingers, while Button knelt before her, carefully drawing the silk stockings on to her feet and smoothing them nicely up the leg. Then her mother would rise, and, standing in her chemise, would allow the maid to fit the long stays of pink coutil, heavily boned, round her hips and slender figure, fastening the busk down the front, after many adjustments; then the suspenders would be clipped to the stockings; then the lacing would follow, beginning at the waist and travelling gradually up and down, until the necessary proportions had been achieved. The silk laces and their tags would fly out, under the maid's deft fingers, with the flick of a skilled worker mending a net. Then the pads of pink satin would be brought, and fastened into place on the hips and under the arms, still further to accentuate the smallness of the waist. Then the drawers; and then the petticoat would be spread into a ring on the floor, and Lucy would step into it on her high-heeled shoes, allowing Button to draw it up and tie the tapes. Then Button would throw the dressing-gown round her shoulders again—Viola had followed the process well, for here the door opened, and the duchess emerged.

Lucy proceeds to be fastened into her dress, ties a diamond dog-collar round her neck, gives her hair a final pat and stands complete: a vision of graceful curves, pouch-fronted and smooth-hipped, sparkling with jewellery and swathed in yards of taffeta, tulle and lace. The Edwardians loved lace; Lucy's petticoat and chemise would have dripped with it. 'There is something very attractive', ran a comment reported by fashion historian C. Willett Cunnington, 'about the elaborate petticoat with its frou-frouing mysteries. Our countrywomen realise at last that dainty undergarments are not necessarily a sign of depravity.'

Now for the 1930s. The lady in question, my informant explains, was

really rather stout—a big, imposing woman—so she needed quite a lot in the way of underpinnings. With the dresses of that time, the least bulge showed unmercifully. Corsets were expensive, though: they were very well made, out of a sort of woven elastic, and you expected to spend easily as much on them as you would on a dress—on a whole outfit, even. The one she had made to go with one of her evening dresses—it was made of blue chiffon, and had almost no back at all—must have cost a *fortune*.

The informant, who, being blessedly skinny, was able to spend her money on frillier items, goes on:

She could, in fact, get dressed without any help at all: her corset did up under the arm, and so did the dress. She just liked having someone to check that her shoulderstraps weren't showing. She'd deal with her underwear and stockings—silk ones, naturally; they cost 15/– a pair and I don't know how many pairs she had—and then I held her dress while she got into it. Her hair was already done, with a permanent wave and a little bun at the back, and she didn't wear much make-up, except powder; so all she had to do then was put on her jewellery. That was all there was to it.

In the three decades that divided these two styles of self-preparation, the most astonishing things had happened to the appearance of a fashionable woman. The high neck (of which the dog-collar was the evening equivalent; it had been invented by Queen Alexandra to hide the scar left from an illness in her youth) gave way to a low scooped line; the figure lost first its S-curve and then all curves whatsoever; the 'rats' were thrown away, back-combing became a lost art, and hair was bobbed, shingled and cropped; and skirts, for the first time in Western civilisation since classical Sparta, rose to a level just short of the knee. 'It seemed', said an inter-war commentator with much approval,

that fashion and common sense were at last synonymous. Clothes so simple in line that the competent home dress-maker could produce passable imitations of Paris models; hats so simple in shape that the working girl's cheap felt was at a distance scarcely distinguisable from her social superior's velour creation; the democratisation of fashion was complete.

But, she goes on sadly, no sooner had this desirable state of things been achieved than long skirts and fashion snobbery began to creep in again: the well-off wore 'elaborate flowing evening creations of the fashion dictators [which] were well beyond the powers of successful imitation of the most accomplished home dressmaker'.

But that, of course, was the whole point. At first glance, the differences between the Edwardian duchess's clothes and those of her '30s counterpart may seem huge: the style, the materials, the sheer quantity of cloth involved. In fact, the biggest difference is less obvious; by the 1930s dressing no longer demanded the services of a second party. ('You can't believe', runs my observer's comment, 'how wonderful it was. The fastenings under the arm meant that you could dress yourself: it was the beginning of your independence.') Otherwise, it was a straight case of *plus ça change*. To display her superior social status, Lucy used her jewellery, her professionally-arranged hair, her dress, the seductive swish made by the petticoat beneath it, the fashionably moulded shape of her figure. (The fact that—as any woman who saw her would know—she could not have got dressed at all without a maid's help was an additional weapon.) The glitter of her '30s counterpart was provided by, again, her jewellery, her hair, her dress, her neatly-restrained ('it must have cost a fortune') hips and bottom. Only the frothing petticoat was missing, since the dress had its own built-in slip; to make up for it, the wearer's ego was much boosted by the knowledge that her sheer stockings, invisible though they might be under her dress, were impeccable.

In methods obvious or subtle—and some of them were very subtle indeed—a lady participant in the social calendar owed it to herself, her husband and her status in society to carry her wealth on her back. And, whatever materials were allowed her by the mode of the day, she faithfully made good her debt.

There are several theories about what makes women's fashion tick. One is based on the straightforward issue of sex appeal: a fashionable woman of a given moment is drawing men's attention to her waist/legs/breasts/bottom/ankles/other part of her anatomy by means of a policy of baring all, provocative concealment or exaggeration. Against this, there is the argument that clothes reflect the spirit of the times. In periods of great social upheaval, so part of the theory runs, women discard the hour-glass look and corsets alike; the Regency period and the 1920s both illustrate the point. A third argument, and one supported by Doris Langley Moore (a fashion historian of great authority in her own right), is double-barrelled: change in dress occurs naturally in societies 'where the existing order may be challenged and the individual will asserted, and where one class or one sex may emulate or vie with another'. A social class which is being imitated, Mrs Langley Moore goes on, seeks to frustrate its imitators by devising new modes and trying to make them hard to copy . . . . Thus in *La Belle Assemblée* we read: 'The more wealthy classes of Society are constantly devising new modes of marking the artificial distinction between themselves and those who are not rich in worldly possessions by a difference in dress.'

La Belle Assemblée was a nineteenth-century equivalent of *Vogue*; shorn of its elegant phrasing, the statement merely repeats the principle always honoured by those who have made it to the top of keeping one step ahead of the aspirant Jones's.

While there is not space here to attempt to catalogue fully the changes that overtook women's fashions between 1837 and 1939, it is interesting to see just how far female upper-classdom managed to stay ahead of 'those who are not rich' by ringing the changes on their clothes—and how far those clothes fit the other two theories mentioned above.

The early Victorian, with her ringlets, bonnets, sloping shoulders, narrow waist and yards of skirt held out by yards of petticoat, fitted the then current feminine ideal of flower-like helplessness. The cut of her sleeves made all but the least energetic arm movements impossible; her tiny slippers pinched; her tight stays made sure that Victorian swoons were things of fact rather than fiction. Every inch of her hand-sewn, hand-trimmed, hand-laundered clothes spoke of conspicuous consumption, while her refined immobility was a status symbol in itself. Only the well-to-do, the newly 'genteel', could afford a daughter who sat on sofas all day.

By contrast, her successor of the 1850s and '60s was a much livelier creature. The crinoline of wire hoops took her skirts out to their ultimate fullness but allowed her to walk more freely. 'Oh, it was delightful,' remembered Gwen Raverat's Aunt Etty. 'I've never been so comfortable since they went out. It kept your petticoats away from your legs, and made walking so light and easy.' The mid-Victorian Miss showed her under-frills, even her ankles; she went swimming in a real purpose-designed bathing-dress; she played croquet in a specially looped-up skirt, whose draperies signalled a fashion for the future. She took to wearing a hat, wide sleeves, a blouse and jacket.

Conspicuous consumption was still hugely apparent, but

trouble was on the way. The wire for crinolines could be mass-produced (in 1859 Sheffield was turning out enough for half a million 'cages' a week), and the home-dressmaker would soon be immeasurably helped in her efforts to vie with the professionals by the introduction of the sewing-machine. Given hindsight, the result seems inevitable. The clothes of the period 1866 to 1880, says Willett Cunnington, give the impression that the 'costumier was indulging in sheer bravura display, inventing new difficulties in order to show her skill in overcoming them.' With the arrival of the bustle, the tied-back skirt and the bustle again, the Society lady became positively overloaded with froth and frills and flounces. The social aspirers would, so the message ran, be thus discouraged, the boundaries between the classes kept clear, and women who were beginning to flirt with emancipation rather than with men be shamed back into proper behaviour. On this last count, fashion lost hands down; it was the 'New Woman's' stiff tailor-mades that, in the last part of the century, set a pronounced day-time fashion of their own.

The emphasis gradually shifted from the posterior to the shoulders: the bustle was followed by the leg-of-mutton sleeve, which could be covered by nothing more practical than a short 'lampshade' cape. After that, the whole outline changed to the softer, smoother curves of the Edwardian period—which, despite their simpler appearance, were more expensive than ever. 'The rich and beautiful brocades, the fine velvets and lustrous satins which made the highest ideal of a costly court train of ten or fifteen years ago', runs a 1907 opinion collected by James Laver,

> did not cost nearly as much as the elaborate hand embroideries of the moment's ambition. It is impossible in either words or black-and-white pictures to give an adequate idea of the beauty of these embroideries. The flowers depicted by the needle are as effective in the mass, as delicate and dainty in minute detail, as their natural prototypes. From a distance evening gowns seem a mass of silver, opalescent gold, or moonlight sequins.

It was a technique that the designers of the post-war 1920s were to find useful: close examination would show that, unlike its passable imitation, the 1920s evening dress was covered with intricate beading or trimming; and it was accompanied by jewellery that might have lost its ornate Edwardian settings but still featured the Edwardian stones. At all stages along the line, from the wilting Miss of the 1840s to the Charleston expert of the cocktail era, the upper-class lady had successfully preserved her superiority against all comers. That her imitators might be unaware of this fact didn't matter; her equals all knew the difference between the sham and the genuine article and acted on the information accordingly.

What, meanwhile, about men? By contrast, says Mrs Langley Moore, the trend of masculine clothing in the nineteenth and twentieth centuries has been 'increasingly towards the path of uniformity'. Female leaders of fashion might shift from bonnet to hat, full skirt to straight skirt, rustling taffeta to whispering lace (a rustling petticoat by the turn of the century was thought vulgar by upper-class experts); but their husbands were content to stick to a costume that varied remarkably little in essentials. These were the shirt, with waistcoat and stock, cravat or tie; the hat and coat; and straight trousers (the Georgian knee-breeches had now become the 'professional' formal wear of either courtiers or liveried servants). The real newcomer was the short, so-called 'lounge' jacket, which turned up in the mid-nineteenth century. This would in the end displace the skirted coat for all but the most formal of dress: the vestigial skirt on the morning coat still worn for weddings nowadays is one of its last survivals. Colours were mainly dark and neutral, and modifications in line and detail were nothing like as sharp as those which overtook women's dresses from one year to the next.

The wives, daughters and mothers of the period—a period during most of which social intercourse took place according to an intensely formalised pattern—had every chance of using their clothes to help them to play the part required; how could men follow their example? That they could and did was in part thanks to the far-reaching pattern set by the Regency Beau Brummell who, a contemporary commented, was 'the quietest, plainest, and most unpretentious dresser . . . his clothes were exquisitely made and, above all, adapted to his person; but for all this there was no striving for effect.' Brummell's own recipe was 'no perfumes but very fine linen, plenty of it, and country washing'. Another factor was the way in which the social calendar added its own dictates to those of the tailors. The nuances were infinite: in the Edwardian period, for example, the frock-coat was proper, the tail-coat more fashionable. A tweed suit was correct wear for the country—but not all the time. 'On some occasions,' Lady Colin Campbell advises, 'neither the tweed costume nor the evening dress suit would be appropriate, but the intermediate dress should be worn—a suit such as is usually donned on Sundays either in town or country—black frock-coat, coloured trousers, and dark tie or scarf.' The wearing of gloves alone was full of intricacies: they were worn when paying a call, when driving or riding and when in church; they were worn in the street and at a ball, but not at a dinner; they were not *usually* worn in the country. A great show of jewellery was deprecated; so, in the more ironclad circles, were racy innovations. The homeric battles between the incomparable Jeeves and poor Bertie mirror the struggle that, well into the inter-war period, took place between a young man's sense of enterprise and his feelings of sartorial duty. 'No, Jeeves,' Bertie says,

'argument is useless. Nobody has a greater respect than I have for your judgment in socks, in ties, and—I will go farther—in spats; but when it comes to evening shirts your nerve seems to fail you. You have no vision. You are prejudiced and reactionary. Hidebound is the word that suggests itself. It may interest you to learn that when I was at Le Touquet the Prince of Wales buzzed into the Casino one night with soft silk shirt complete. When we Woosters are adamant, we are—well, adamant.'

But Jeeves wins in the end: Bertie is not to be allowed—now or ever—to desert the standards that his position in society demands.

For women, naturally, the rules were even more complicated. A simple morning dress for mornings at home; a slightly smarter morning dress for paying calls to close friends in the morning; a sober afternoon dress for paying 'morning' (afternoon) calls on foot; a much grander affair, with a lace sunshade, for paying calls in a carriage; a tweed suit for the country (but *not* for church); a tea-gown, all lace and draperies; a lavish dinner dress (with a high neck if the wearer were to dine at a restaurant); an even more lavish ball-gown—these were the basics, and the basics only, of an Edwardian lady's wardrobe. There was also the endless paraphernalia of hats, gloves, shoes, stockings, parasols, fans, jewellery, boas and motoring coats. It is unsurprising that, as Lady Cynthia Asquith commented, 'we were forever changing our clothes.'

Then, too, there were the niceties involved in actually wearing it all. This was a matter that went far beyond the adage 'you can tell a lady by her gloves and her boots.' It was, for instance, the height of vulgarity in the nineteenth century to let your train sweep the outdoor pavement (though not the indoor carpet); but picking it up was also fraught with peril. The right way, Willett Cunnington reports, was to grasp the skirt delicately between the fingers and lift it up on one hip, 'resting the hand on the hip without turning the elbow out'. It is remarkably difficult to hold a dress up like this while keeping the elbow tucked in: hence, of course, the inherent attraction of the procedure. It would be the unknowing, the jumped-up, the all too *nouvelle riche* who let her elbow stick out like a jug handle.

And there was still one further eventuality that demanded a close alliance between the rules of fashion and those of etiquette. It was death. At the height of the Victorian cult of mourning, a widow wore mourning for three years, the first of which was spent in unornamented black, covered with crepe. In the second, she could leave off her widow's cap, along with some of the crepe, and wear jet jewellery. In the third, she could add touches of mauve or grey. Mourning was worn for a year if a parent or child died; for less in the case of other relatives (just how much less demanded an exquisite sense of social propriety). Children could wear white clothes with black trimmings; servants—if it was the head of the household who had died—were given black gloves and black work dresses.

All the family mourners secluded themselves from social events for a suitable period; a year, in the case of close relatives. For them, Society too had died. That, in their seclusion, they bothered so much about their degrees of mourning dress shows that the habit of demonstrating degree by dress had bitten them to the core.

CHAPTER NINE

〜〜〜

Abroad

Happiness is not complete, however, when one enjoys a fine carriage, a well-appointed home, regular occupation, a seat in Parliament, and the prospect of a seat in Paradise; for amid all these good things, there are times when one yawns and feels depressed. Then the luggage is got ready, one steps on board a steamer, and proceeds in quest of change, of something to distract one's thoughts of a glimpse of the sun.

Hippolyte Taine,
Notes on England;
third English edition, 1872

They were armouring their minds against this filthy country, sticking pins into human dummies to exorcise the unspeakable things that crouched in every corner of their real lives.

John Masters,
Nightrunners of Bengal, 1951

A small handbook published in 1873 entitled *How to Dress on £15 a Year as a Lady—by a Lady* devoted the whole of its last chapter to travel abroad. The advice it gives is both charming and sensible: travel with as little luggage as possible; be ruthlessly economical in your choice of accessories ('the same sashes will then do to wear with all your dresses'); carry a warm jacket for the Channel crossing; avoid long-handled umbrellas, as they 'catch in other people's legs and packages, to your own and their great discomfort'.

On the question of actual dresses, the anonymous author is more sensible still. She suggests taking only two for 'best' wear.

A prettily made black and white silk (the latter colour predominating), nicely trimmed with flat flounces of the same (no *ruches,* for they crush in packing) you would find extremely useful. The silk itself need not be expensive, provided it is bright and soft, and fashionably cut. It would do afterwards for a demi-toilette dinner dress at home. Your second good dress might be a cream-coloured washing silk . . . which is especially suited for a traveller, as it packs into a wonderfully small compass, and shakes out as fresh as possible. You should have both dresses made open, square or V-shaped in front, so that they could be worn for either morning or evening.

Interestingly, she finds that white dresses keep clean quite as long as and are less troublesome than coloured ones; washing and cleaning, of course, are done by hotel staff for a fee—an 'extravagant' one, the author says crossly. For travelling and walking, however, brown holland is recommended.

Flounces and all, Victorian dresses do pack reasonably flat; the array described above, plus one white dress 'for walking in the gardens before breakfast', plus the accompanying sashes, stockings and underwear, is intended to fit into *half* a small basket trunk, thirty inches by twenty by sixteen. Half, because the author is envisaging the likely case of two genteel but slightly impoverished sisters travelling together: travelling, as she hypothesises, 'for the three or four summer months, to Germany, Switzerland, the Tyrol'; stopping for a while at Baden-Baden, Homburg or 'an equally fashionable watering-place'; wearing their best silk dresses 'at the Kursaal in the evening, or at the concert and other amusements, which are constantly going on at all these places'; and then, perhaps, rounding off their holiday with a 'scrambling tour in Switzerland', on which the brown holland will come in useful. (So will red rather than white cotton drawers, 'for, should they be accidentally seen—and this is sometimes unavoidable in mountain expeditions—they look much nicer'.)

The Victorians, when the urge took them, were tremendous travellers. The difference between these two lively if hypothetical spinsters, jollying off on their vacation, and Marianne North, who visited Canada, Jamaica, Brazil, Sarawak, Ceylon, Australia, Honolulu and Chile on a botanical mission that lasted a lifetime, was one of degree only. A lot of the travelling, certainly, was done in the name of God, but most amateur travellers stuck to the simple aim of combining pleasure with a little improvement of mind or body. It was basically in the name of improvement that, from the Tudor period onwards, scions of the British aristocracy had been sent off on the Grand Tour; the trip would, it was hoped, brush up their culture, polish their manners, bring them into contact with equals among the European ruling class and return them to England groomed and ready to take their place among the country's rulers. Some, having taken to the pleasurable aspects of Abroad, showed a marked reluctance to do this; in the eighteenth century, the Duke of Kingston stayed away from his native shores for no less than ten years.

The Grand Tour was an expensive affair; Kingston spent £40,000 on his decade-long junket. But the notion that no education was complete without a spell abroad was still going strong by the time Hippolyte Taine arrived in England, at which point travel had become accessible to people of much more moderate means. 'I know one', he writes, 'who, having several children, and making some £500 a year, annually deducts from this moderate income £40 for an excursion.' At the same time, the fact-finding tour had become well established. When their lengthy holidays came round, MPs vanished to France, Spain, Italy, Germany to collect data, opinion and impressions. 'One of them', Taine says with a faint hint of derision,

> goes to our farms, examines the manure, the implements, the cattle, makes a collection of statistics, and, on his return, prints or delivers a series of lectures on the state of agriculture in France. Another one surveys the Paris manufactories, whilst his wife visits the professional schools. Below the statesman, nearly all the rich or merely well-off people do likewise.

It would, however, have to be an exceptionally dedicated fact-finder who continually denied himself a trip to the great leisure centres of Europe. Up to the middle of the nineteenth century, these tended to be the German spas; later, when gambling was forbidden there, the pendulum of fashion swung to France and Monaco. But Baden, Homburg and the rest continued to retain a fashionable place in the British social calendar, for the prosaic reason that Society, having eaten its head off from the autumn through to August, now needed a place and a time in which its system could be

de-coked. 'Bath-chairs', Grenville Murray notes in 1881, 'are
not an enlivening feature in the gardens of the Kursaals.
Nevertheless, the beautiful scenery remains, and the bands
of music, and the attraction of an occasional crowned head,
who comes with a large suite, and causes crowds of
aristocratic families to come also.'

He goes on to point out that the spas are a great place for
the married gad-about to commence operations: the lack of
people who know her, the crowds of people who don't and
the general atmosphere of here today, gone tomorrow are all
conducive to having 'all the fun she wants'. For an
unmarried girl, the business was more serious, since Ems,
Homburg and Marienbad provided an ideal post-Season
terrain for husband-hunting. (In another sense, Abroad also
provided a girl with her last chance. If her parents, for
reasons of social disgrace or economy, were forced to retire
to the Continent, she focused her intentions sharply on other
British residents or holiday-makers and did all she could to
catch one. An alternative was to go completely native and
marry into the foreign community in which she found
herself.)

Homburg was particularly attractive, as was Marienbad;
they were the favourite resorts of the Prince of Wales and his
set, and a presentation to royalty could be fairly easily
arranged here. The Prince's main business, like that of all the
serious spa visitors, was the observance of a strict regime, the
main components of which were diet, exercise and the
'waters'. Diet was probably the easiest part of it: a Homburg
menu presented as typical in a 1903 *Gourmet's Guide to
Europe* started with carrot soup and continued with trout,
tongue, roast capon, salad and peach pudding. Exercise, too,
lacked terror; it could, according to Grenville Murray,
consist of 'a quick march through the gardens, or out into the
country among the woods and fields of maize'. But the
waters were different.

At Ems, for example, the shrinking health-fiends would
turn up at the appointed times and join the crowd round a
small, railed enclosure with a pool inside. Inside the railing,
on the 'waters' very edge, stood two female spa attendants in
caps and aprons; one was armed with a long scoop, while the
other handed out the scoop's contents. Come your turn, you
were given a cupful of something that not only tasted
horribly of steel but was also lukewarm. The most

faint-hearted can only have been kept going by the prospect
of oyster omelet, roast hare and supreme of pheasant with
chestnut purée that would replace the carrot soup when they
got home.

For the really determined travellers among Britain's
leisured classes, the only part of the year that needed to be
spent at home—really at home, as opposed to a rented house
in London—was autumn. Those with a long list of friends
could alleviate the horrors of this by embarking on a tight
schedule of country-house visiting, combined with shooting
and hunting. After Christmas, in the same winter quest for
the sun that takes the rich of today on cruises, the travellers
would return to the Continent and throw themselves into the
South of France Season, which lasted until mid-May. Then
the London Season took over, to be followed by the spa
Season again. It was a programme, said a significant passage
in the *Graphic* of 1907, that governed the movements of
'several hundreds of men and women in England, whose
main object in this direction is to keep apart from the
majority'.

Queen Victoria herself joined the late winter exodus: she
received the notorious Sarah Bernhardt at Nice, was bullied
by John Brown into a Balmoral regime at Cannes and,
bullying notwithstanding, thoroughly enjoyed herself. 'I
shall mind returning to the sunless north,' she wrote after a
visit to Cimiez in 1899, her last, as it turned out, overseas.
But, for many of her subjects and—more especially—for
those of her son, the real attractions of the Riviera were not
the warm sunshine, the battle of the flowers at Nice or the
gentle stroll along the Promenade des Anglais; they were the
terrifying joys of Monte Carlo, where the ordinary gambling
unit was a *mille*, worth about £40. Monte Carlo in its Season
was the centre, not merely of the European upper classes,
but of the world's. Super-rich Americans came over to
Europe on board the *Caronia* and the *Carmania*; Russian
princes, once the mid-winter Season at their own court was
over, entrained on the St Petersburg–Vienna–Cannes
express and dressed for dinner during the journey. A few
preferred Biarritz, where the English influence was so strong
as to have brought about the creation of one of the more
remarkable hunts in history, the Biarritz and Bayonne
Foxhounds. But the pull of Monte Carlo's gaming-tables
sooner or later made itself felt. 'Even those who do not

frankly love them are attracted,' wrote Lady Helen Forbes in the *Queen* of 1905. 'They hover near with a fearful joy. Their vanity is flattered by the idea that they are doing something wicked and daring, and they speak of their exploits with a self-conscious laugh. "Of course, it is a dreadful place, you know. I only went there to see how horrid it was." '

For their pains, the terrified gloaters found themselves enmeshed in one of the highest cost-of-living rates in Europe; an ordinary restaurant charged prices comparable with those of London's Savoy Hotel. On the other hand, the camaraderie of money allowed even some of etiquette's most obvious dictates to be passed over. A drawing of the Casino's roulette room in 1902 shows women wearing an astonishingly wide-ranging assortment of clothes: toilettes include full evening-dress (with dog-collar and flowers in the hair); a floppy lace afternoon dress (without dog-collar); several smart day outfits, topped by elegant confections of flowers and feathers; and a blouse and skirt, accompanied by a businesslike straw hat. In the Rooms, the usually rigid rules governing what was worn when did not apply. Men were similarly freed from such restrictions on their wardrobe; the only wear in which they were not allowed to appear was knickerbockers.

Monte Carlo—reigning supreme in fashion at a period when huge personal fortunes coincided with the pre-*Titanic* boom in luxury inter-continental travel—probably presented the world with its first true forerunner of the Jet Set. But the trend that would make the jetsetters of the second half of the twentieth century head in winter and spring for the snowline, rather than the Mediterranean, had already been born. Its origins were similar to those that had brought both the spas and the Riviera into prominence: health combined with a little fun. True, Switzerland did not offer much in the way of built-in worldly amusements, but it did have snow, sun, good hotels, clear air and tobogganing. These facilities were all its own; it was left to the British—always ready, as the Biarritz Foxhounds showed, to start sports where none had existed before—to introduce the final attraction. Towards the end of the nineteenth century, a few tweed-suited enthusiasts learnt to ski in Norway, enjoyed the activity and brought it south.

In the Edwardian period, the Alpine resorts of Wengen,

Gstaad, Davos and Adelboden took off; by the 1920s the switch from balmy sea breezes to snow had developed far enough for *Punch* to make it cruelly clear that Monte Carlo's clientele had become somewhat suburban, while Mentone was full of retired colonels. Winter sports, by now, were *the* thing to go in for, although an alternative winter possibility was the long-standing one of Egypt.

Meanwhile, the time for coastlines and beaches became more firmly fixed than ever at high summer. There was, of course, nothing particularly new about spending August at the seaside (even Cowes, after all, counts as the seaside), but the interwar period added a new and important ingredient to the summer holiday: the sun tan. The cult of the sun—another of the unprecedented revolutions that overtook fashion in the wake of the First World War—had arrived and with it the need to be in as constant and as hot a sun as possible. Clearly, the German spas did not quite fit the bill. Nor yet did England itself. 'Perfectly sickening!' laments an odious *Punch* poppet of the '20s. 'All my friends are at Deauville or the Lido, and here am I stranded on the South Coast . . . it's too noisome to be *nowhere.*'

Although a cruise was, strictly speaking, 'nowhere', the idea of one would not have produced the same lacklustre response; a cruise in the Mediterranean in someone's private yacht would have fulfilled her wildest dreams. For the less well connected but still wealthy sun-hunters, there were always the commercial cruises. After a wobbly start in the nineteenth century, by the Roaring Twenties cruising had suddenly caught on. Ship after ship was purpose built as, or converted into, a luxury full-time cruiser; the most popular of them all was the Blue Star Line's *Arandora Star,* which had started out life as a refrigerated meat-transporter. When made over, she boasted not only a ballroom, garden lounge and gym but also an open-air pool and a sports deck eighty feet long by sixty.

To British Society, Abroad had meant, more or less successively, a leisurely trip round Europe, viewing places and people of interest; a gathering of the clans, in Germany and on the Riviera; a faith, adhered to in the face of all reason, that the luck of the tables must turn in the end; a tumble down a snowy mountain; and lizard-like basking, equipped with two-piece bathing-dress and cocktail shaker,

somewhere in the sun. But what about the hundreds of
thousands of people for whom Abroad represented work?
Or for whom, indeed, Abroad was England? A 'Society'
existed in all of them, along with a social calendar; but,
especially in the Dominions, the individual forms and quirks
that developed would have shaken a British Society matron
into speechlessness. In New Zealand, for example, the hub of
the social calendar—with its balls, débutantes, At Homes and
the rest—was Government House, Wellington. The dances
given there carried the greatest prestige of any. But getting
an invitation to a Government House party, prestigious
though it was, presented a quite startling lack of difficulty:
you simply signed your name in the Visitors' Book and
waited for the square of pasteboard to arrive. In Australia,
the man-about-town of Melbourne had to dress *down* rather
than up for his Sunday afternoon stroll: a top hat, gloves and
a white waistcoat (all of them so ordinary amongst Top
Victorians in England as to not merit a second glance) would
earn him a disagreeable degree of attention from groups of
flashily clad 'larrikins' whose 'overheard fragments of
conversation among themselves [were] quite offensive
enough'. The passage is quoted from an 1886 number of the
Australian Review by Asa Briggs in his study of Victorian
cities; he points out that an important difference between
Melbourne and a British equivalent was that the Australian
well-to-do class 'showed little instinctive understanding for
the delicate nuances of English social status, although it had a
cliquishness and a marked stratification of its own'.

British visitors did not care for such overriding of their
most cherished social regulations; they would have preferred
the social atmosphere of New Zealand, which was, on the
whole, more genteel, more 'English'. But even the most
determined attempts at gentility had, there as everywhere
else in what is now the Commonwealth, a way of picking up
characteristics that owed considerably more to the frontier
spirit than to the parent culture. New Zealand ladies, for
example, thought nothing of paying their formal calls on
foot (tea was served on these occasions; the visitors, some of
whom might have walked several miles, would have needed
it). Girls in the crinoline period made their crinolines out of
hoops of stiff vine when wire was unobtainable. Social
gatherings, once actually gathered, went on for a
considerable time: one dance lasted a night, a day and

another night. Ladies travelled with a pistol stuck in their garter for protection against emergencies.

Lack of servants, lack of female society, lack of the amenities that the upholders of the English social calendar took for granted: these, together with a deliberately-cultivated democratic ideal, were some of the factors that lay behind the New Zealand ladies' compromises between the demands of polite society and those of their circumstances. The social and emotional link between them and Britain was a loose one: there was no full-scale coming and going of official personnel from England to reinforce English social patterns; no sense of the native millions outside the social pale, against whom a rigid adherence to these patterns might serve as a barrier. (Relations with the Maoris, which in 1860 had exploded into war, eased again relatively quickly; in 1867, New Zealand's original inhabitants were given parliamentary representation.) The opposite was true of the colonies. Amenities might be lacking; so might women. But the sense of 'Home'— England—was there in force, as were the servants. The business of dressing for dinner in the jungle, so old a joke that it has now lost all its humour, was no joke then; it was a comforting reminder that Home, and its standards, still existed.

British India, the possession that in 1876 gave Victoria her double title of *Regina et Imperatrix*, presented the most elaborate case of this 'dressing for dinner' syndrome. In a sense, the whole place was a jungle, in which the Clubs, the cantonments, the bungalows where memsahibs and their gardeners tried to grow British flowers, the up-country stations and the hill resorts were mere clearings, always in danger of being re-possessed by the undergrowth.

To keep those clearings inhabitable, the British Raj employed the strong will of its womenfolk and extraordinary quantities of hired labour. This was abundant to a degree far in excess of what the average officer-class family could have afforded at home, and numbers were increased by the complications of the caste system. Thus, the lowest rank among the living-in domestics was occupied by an untouchable sweeper, whose job was to empty the lavatory or 'thunderbox' after it had been used. Between his brief spells of work, he would spend his day waiting on the veranda. Gardening was carried out on a similar labour-intensive scale: one memory, collected by the BBC for their radio series on British India, features a party of three or four men who 'would spread out with a yard or two between them and go up and down the lawn on their hunkers, each man picking out a weed, with another man behind him with a basket, egging him on'. Even further complexities were noted by sisters Jon and Rumer Godden, whose childhood was spent mainly in Bengal:

> If a crow fell dead in our garden or one of our guinea-pigs died, Nitai, our sweeper, could not pick up or touch the corpse; a boy of a special sect had to be called in from the bazaar; he put on his best shirt of marigold-coloured silk to do this grisly work.

British Society in India revolved round two major factors: the physical seasons and the Club. It was the seasons—cold, hot or wet—that dictated the pattern that the Raj's social calendar took, while the Club did much of the rest. Any centre except the smallest had its Club: in title, a polo or gymkhana club, but in actuality a social centre for the élite of the European element resident in the locality. Joining the local Club was an important step in the process of being accepted in an area; eligibility stopped, more or less, at the lower limit of the upper-middle class, and non-eligibility meant social non-existence as far as Society was concerned. Once accepted, however, members were all set for the legendary Raj routine of polo, chota pegs, bridge, gossip, shikar and dances.

The pace stepped up in the period before Christmas: this, the best part of the November-to-April 'cold season', was also the Raj's own Season, when the closely-packed dances, parties and sporting events were adorned by the newly-arrived representatives of the Fishing Fleet. (The Fishing Fleet was the collective name given to all the girls with family connections in India who came out with a view to catching husbands.) It reached an early climax at Christmas (with pea-fowl rather than turkey and presents ordered from Home in October) and New Year. New Year's Day was marked by military parades, with cavalry, elephants and bands. After that, the tempo slowed: a final grand event—the Viceroy's Ball at Delhi—carried the ominous message that the hot weather, with its temperatures of 130 degrees in the shade, would shortly begin.

The hot weather was hell, and the rains that followed it almost worse. 'In East India Company days,' say the Goddens, 'the rains were called the sickly season, a time for dysentery, boils and fevers, particularly the abominable dengue or seven days' fever that made bones ache worse than influenza, heads throb, skins tender. That year, we children had all these among us.' It was not surprising that all those members of Raj Society who could get away escaped to the hill stations. They were, just like their counterparts in Britain, aiming for the usual holiday goal of health and a little fun. Since the women, for obvious reasons, were in the majority at the hill stations, the fun to be obtained there was the sort of fun they liked: parties, with all the rules of precedence in full force; amateur theatricals, with cut-throat competition for the best parts and the best bouquets; jockeying for social power; and flirtation. The male atmosphere of hard drinking, hard riding and hard work was left down on the Plains: Simla, Musoorie, Darjeeling, Ootacamund in the south were very much a woman's—a European woman's—world, organised along the lines of the April-to-July 'ladies' game' at Home.

In October, the memsahibs and their families left the hills, and in 1947 they got out of India for good. But the mere mention of Simla has still not lost its power to provoke nostalgia or rage—nostalgia for, or rage against, an extraordinary attempt to transplant a whole culture. Both reactions—rage and nostalgia—are linked to the fact that, by and large, the transplant was successful.

Ladies' international skiing race, Austria, 1894

CHAPTER TEN

∾∾∾

Accessories to the Fact

I know it's all dead and gone. Things like that don't happen now. But I think it's worth not forgetting that they did happen.

Margaret Powell,
Below Stairs, 1968

One of the most poignant aspects of the British Raj was home-coming; or, rather, Home-coming. A permanent return to England meant a return to a temperate climate; to food that need not be double-washed, water that need not be boiled; to simple cough-mixture rather than quinine; to a life where no years'-long parting hung over the heads of parents and children. But the relief of Home-coming was mixed with some startling difficulties of adjustment. Little girls like the Goddens promptly had to drop what they called their 'princess' attitudes, and adults had to face a fall in living standards that reduced their social scope from a level that was indeed near-regal to something much more humdrum. And one of the principal factors in this reduction was the instant decrease awaiting Home-comers in the numbers of servants they could afford.

In both India and England, servants were the ultimate key to the social calendar. Without them, the calendar's participants would have had little leisure in which to participate. Without them, the balls, the vast dinners, the incredible perfection of the clothes, the transport between one gathering and the next, the riding, hunting and shooting would simply not have been practical possibilities. Servants, though by no means participants in the social calendar themselves, were still part of it; they were the engine that made the whole thing work.

Of course, the returning memsahib would not have had to make do with no servants at all. In the nineteenth century and the first part of the twentieth, the 'servant-keeping classes' extended not just to the lower limits of upper-middle

103

classdom but way beyond them. Isabella Beeton, in her 1906 *Book of Household Management,* gives the following table of household income matched against servant up-keep.

About £1000 a year............Cook, Housemaid, and
                                    perhaps a man-servant.

From £750-£500 a year.............Cook, Housemaid.

About £300 a year...................General Servant.

About £200 a year.........Young girl for rough work.

These are middle-class households; for those with an income of above £1000 the numbers of servants mounted sharply. It needed to; it was at this point in the income ranges that the pull of the national social calendar began to make itself felt in earnest.

Outside the royal establishments, the top limit of servants kept was probably reached by households of the order of Longleat, which in its Edwardian heyday had a staff of forty-three. 'The intricate hive which buzzed so busily below stairs led a complete life of its own; and its ritual and etiquette make a fascinating study,' wrote Daphne Fielding, former wife of the Marquess of Bath, in 1951. She went on to give a list of the Longleat personnel at the turn of the century: one house steward, one butler, one under-butler; one groom of the chambers, one valet, three footmen, one steward's room footman; two oddmen, two pantry boys, one lamp boy; one housekeeper, two lady's maids, one nurse, one nursery maid; eight housemaids, two sewing maids, two still-room maids, six laundry maids; one chef, two kitchen maids, one vegetable maid, one scullery maid, one daily woman. The king and queen of this below-stairs establishment were the house steward—who did the accounts—and the housekeeper; but the real money-earner was the chef. In the 1880s, for example, he earnt £130 a year, as against the housekeeper's £60.

On top of that, there were fourteen 'outdoor' servants working in the stables: they included 'a coachman, a second coachman, a carriage groom, a steel boy (whose duty was to burnish the bits and metal parts of the harness) and a "tiger", a small boy in livery who sat upright on the box of the carriage, his arms folded stiffly on his chest'. It should be pointed out that the minimum school leaving age at the end of the nineteenth century was twelve. As will be seen later, a child's own parents were the main supporters of his immediate entry into employment.

It goes without saying that the life of a 'lower' servant was insupportably hard by today's standards (the 'upper' servants—the butler, the housekeeper, the lady's maids and the valets—formed a sort of officer class). The days started at six or even earlier; the personal accommodation was in dismally meagre contrast with the comfort of the employing family's apartments. An editorial reply to a letter sent to the *Ladies' Treasury* in 1867 suggests that a servant should have an iron bedstead, two inexpensive wool mattresses, unbleached cotton sheets to be changed every fortnight and—as a special luxury—a feather pillow. This, however, is an exception to the writer's general rule: 'Remember,' the reply goes on, 'to be careful of a servant's health and comfort; but indulgence is not apt to improve her health, temper or manners.'

But it was the servants at the very bottom of the scale—those unfortunate enough to be in the lower-income households and therefore at the receiving end of every one of the mistress's orders—who were used to a brutally harsh degree. Some of those 'young girls for rough work' were eleven-year-olds in their first place, which they had to keep for a year; treatment varied from kindly to abysmal.

In a house with several servants, however, matters improved—not because the employer was necessarily better-hearted but because the strict demarcation zones that applied to servants' work could start to operate. 'Each [servant] has his post rigorously defined,' says Taine in the 1860s. 'The work is divided, no one either trespasses on, or trusts to another.' As an example, he quotes an eighteen-servant house which, almost living up to British Raj standards, had a 'special man for sweeping, carrying coal, lighting and keeping up the fires'. With this rigorous system of job definition came possibility of not merely an occasional pause in the day's work but of the chance during that pause to consider oneself an individual human being. 'The servants retain their independence, and they cleave to it,' Taine goes on.

In London many of them have a club, an association whereof the members agree not to continue longer than two consecutive years in the same house; this is in order to leave less power to the masters. Moreover, as their hours are regulated, they are their own masters during the intervals of their service. They have their own hall, a large room wherein they take their meals and sit. In the [eighteen-servant] house of which I spoke, their dinner and their breakfast are served half an hour before those of their masters. They have a small library for their use, draughts, chess; after dinner they may go out; one only is kept to answer the bell.

As the Longleat list indicates, the range of specialised servants' jobs could be expanded almost indefinitely. Indeed, some of the footmen had super-specialised roles: one worked exclusively for the nursery, another for the Marchioness. The groom of the chambers looked after the reception rooms, communications and the needs of visitors. There had also once been a courier, who acted as a sort of private travel agent. But, in almost any household that employed a total staff of more than four, certain broad areas of demarcation were apparent. The great gulf was between indoor and outdoor staff; hostesses thinking of bringing in one of the grooms to act as a temporary waiter at table were warned that they did so at their peril. The outdoor staff was divided into those who looked after the grounds and those who looked after the horses or, later, the cars. The indoor group was more complicated; by and large, indoor servants grouped themselves into the categories of kitchen department, housework, 'front of the house' and executive (the lady's maids and nannies were in super-specialised categories of their own).

'Front of the house' domestics were those whose jobs brought them into direct contact with their employers and their friends. The parlourmaid (who, in more modest households, did much of the work that a grand establishment would have allotted to male staff) answered the door and the bells; laid, and waited at, table; served tea. Menservants had a similar schedule but also had to give general tone to the scene: footmen were frequently matched for size, like horses. They all, obviously, had endless behind-the-scenes tasks as well: 'must understand lamps,' ran one *Morning Post* advertisement for a footman.

The executive group were the butler, the housekeeper

and—in establishments such as Longleat—the steward. The butler was not only the resident consultant on drink, the guardian of the family plate, the dining-room overseer, the announcer of guests and a stand-in valet for his master: he was also, as far as the other servants were concerned, the Wrath of God. 'If a groom should appear with a dirty coat,' Taine explains, 'his master says nothing to him, but reprimands the butler.' The reprimand would then be handed on to the real offender. The housekeeper, if there were one, ruled the women staff in the same way; it was she who organised the labour available, controlled standards and supplies and guarded morals. She was also the arbiter on below-stairs etiquette, which in a Society household paralleled that of the drawing-room in complexity. In the grandest households of all, the upper servants dined separately from the rest of their colleagues, in evening dress; the question of which visiting lady's maid should be taken to dinner by the head resident manservant was decided according to the maid's employer's status. Thus, it would be the maid to the wife of a Marquess's eldest son who would take the head butler's arm, rather than that of the wife of the younger son of a duke. (In addition—as Miss Sackville-West points out in *The Edwardians*—the valets and maids were actually called after the people they worked for. 'Although the Duchess of Hull's maid had stayed many times at Chevron, and was indeed quite a crony of Mrs Wickenden's, invited to private sessions in the housekeeper's room, where the two elderly gossips sat stirring their cups of tea, she was never known as anything but Miss Hull.')

The housemaids' province was the house itself: its fires, floors, beds, dust-free ornaments, polished surfaces and upstairs supplies of hot water (all of it carried up by hand until plumbing became a practical possibility). The work was made even more arduous by the fact that much of it had to be completed very early in the morning, before the employers arrived on the scene. Beds were made while the 'family' were eating breakfast. Housemaids were not part of the 'front of the house' staff; in some households, those accidentally discovered working in the 'family's' area had to preserve a fiction of invisibility by turning their face to the wall until the discoverer had gone past. The sixth Duke of Portland, an obsessive recluse, reversed the question of who saw whom by threatening to dismiss any workman who touched his hat to him. Housemaids who got caught in the front of the house here had a considerably kinder punishment: they were ordered to do a spell on the special skating rink that the Duke had had built for his servants' amusement.

The most junior housemaid was, in a sense, the most junior servant in the general hierarchy, since kitchen staff were a law to themselves. As Daphne Fielding explains, these were excused morning prayers (which all the other servants in all households naturally attended, in order of strict precedence; the family would also be present in force, and the master of the house would officiate) since they were getting the breakfast. They ate in the kitchen and, according to some accounts, usually slept beside it rather than in the normal servants' quarters high up in the building. And they had a ranking order that paralleled rather than interleaved with the general servants' establishment. At their head was the cook, one of the most important people in the whole house; at the foot was the newest, rawest and hardest-worked servant of all, the scullery-maid. To her fell the kitchen's roughest tasks: the scrubbing, the scouring, the incredible amounts of dish-washing. A child in an upper-class house would often be on good (or at least speaking) terms with the butler, the 'front' staff, the housemaids and the outdoor personnel—but seldom with those of the kitchen. 'We were rather frightened of Cook,' runs one memory from a comparatively modest establishment of the 1920s. 'She was a mysterious figure; we hardly ever saw her at all. We'd catch sight of her just sometimes, in the garden; she had her own way in to the basement, where the kitchen was.'

There is no difficulty in imagining the hardships to which a lower servant of any type was subjected: included among them were gruelling fatigue, boredom, 'industrial hazards' such as the raw-skinned fingers of the scullery-maid and, above all, the near-total lack of anything that we—unlike Taine—could call independence. There could be no closing up shop after a day's work; a servant's home *was* his or her day's work. 'In some ways,' says Margaret Powell, recalling her career below stairs in the inter-war period,

we weren't much better off than serfs, inasmuch as our whole life was regulated by our employers; the hours we worked, the clothes we wore—definitely the clothes we

wore at work, and to some extent the clothes we wore
when we went out. Even our . . . very scanty free time was
over-shadowed by the thought that we 'mustn't be in later
than ten o'clock.'

Nor is it difficult to understand the extremely ambivalent
attitude held by servants towards their employers: affection
and scalding contempt were normally the two extremes, with
all varieties of emotion in between. Surprisingly frequently,
affection won out to the extent that a servant completely
identified him or herself with the employer's family: 'I had
an aunt', says an informant of the 1970s,

who was a housekeeper to the last unmarried daughter of
a titled family. Whenever her sisters visited her she'd
never talk to them about herself; only about the family
she worked for. She'd started there as a housemaid, and
had been there when half of them were born; she knew all
their affairs right down to the last detail. The odd thing
was that, when she ended up as housekeeper, the woman
she worked for adopted her own family in much the same
way—always remembering birthdays and so on.

Mrs Powell, however, has an astringent comment on this
sort of servant-mistress relationship: 'that, of course, was the
kind of servant that people really liked, because if you
submerged your whole personality in your employers, they
were going to get the very best out of you.'

What is difficult is to make the imaginative leap required
to understand why posts in 'service' were not only filled but
coveted. The reason was economic necessity of the most
grinding sort—explained by, among others, Flora
Thompson in Lark Rise to Candleford. In Lark Rise, she
says, there was no girl over twelve who was living at
home; and it was Lark Rise and all its equivalents that
provided servant-keeping houses everywhere with their
scullery-maids. Here is what happened.

As soon as a little girl approached school-leaving age, her
mother would say, 'About time you was earnin' your own
livin', me gal,' or, to a neighbour, 'I shan't be sorry when
our young So-and-So gets her knees under somebody
else's table. Five slices for breakfast this mornin', if you
please!' From that time onward the child was made to feel
herself one too many in the overcrowded home; while her

brothers, when they left school and began to bring home a few shillings weekly, were treated with a new consideration and made much of.

Lark Rise parents did not like their sons leaving; they were the rising generation of wage-earners. But girls, as well as being useless mouths, were also quite literally in the way. In a two-bedroomed cottage, the boys of the family had one room, while 'the girls still at home had to sleep in the parents' room. They had their own standard of decency; a screen was placed or a curtain was drawn to form a partition between the parents' and children's beds; but it was, at best, a poor makeshift arrangement, irritating, cramped, and inconvenient.' The girls had to go, and employment in gentlemen's service was regarded as giving the best—indeed, almost the only—career prospects open to a respectable working-class woman. The scullery-maid's promotion ladder, if she were good at her work, ended at cook or even cook-housekeeper; a housemaid might in the end work directly up to housekeeper status. So, prepared by a year in their locally-held 'first place', the girls went—and found that, as far as food and living conditions were concerned, they had made a reasonably good bargain. It was the rest of the business—and, especially, the extravagant contrasts between upstairs and downstairs—that was very much less than reasonable.

In the inter-war period, a rumbling discontent in the servants' halls began to be heard and then, given the new work openings for women, to make itself felt in practical terms. Employers slowly began to respond to the pressure. But this response was in a short time to be proved vain. Soon, England's resident memsahibs were to face a Home-coming of their own and, in the living conditions that awaited them after the Second World War, the former servants' halls would in all probability be converted into basement flats, shortly to be snapped up by the children of the one-time employers and servants alike. The key to the whole machine—cheap domestic labour—had finally fallen out; labour-saving devices notwithstanding, no true substitute would be found. From now on, only the very wealthy would be able to afford the degree of personal service in the home that had once been taken for granted in much less well-heeled households.

In the 1960s, this writer attended a large, and obviously costly, dance in the Midlands, given at a private house. Until the small hours, servants of all varieties were in attendance; by the morning, they had vanished and were never seen again. The house returned to its normal routine. Food was prepared and eaten in the one-time mysterious territory of the kitchen; the overnight guests drifted out to the lawn to watch the marquee being dismantled. And the hostess—rich though she may have been, glassy-eyed with fatigue though she certainly was—confronted the business of washing up breakfast for ten. In more senses than one, for her the ball was over.

A quiet moment, 1885

CHAPTER ELEVEN

∞∞

Sport

It is recorded that, in the season 1896–97, the Sand-ringham guests shot 13,958 pheasants, 3,965 partridges, 836 hares, 6,185 rabbits, 77 woodcock, 52 teal, 271 wild duck, 18 pigeons, and 27 'various birds'.

Roger Hart,
English Life in the Nineteenth Century, 1971

One task that took place with monotonous regularity below stairs, while below stairs still existed, was the packing of picnic hampers: hampers for race-goers, hampers for shooting-parties, hampers for spectators at Lord's or Henley. A typical inter-war version is described by Bertie Wooster's race-going friend Bingo Little (young Bingo has reasons of his own for knowing what is in this particular lunch): ' "There's ham sandwiches," he proceeded, a strange soft light in his eyes, "and tongue sandwiches and potted meat sandwiches and game sandwiches and hard-boiled eggs and lobster and a cold chicken and sardines and a cake and a couple of bottles of Bollinger and some old brandy." ' A menu for an Ascot picnic, though compiled well before the Wodehouse/Wooster era, is the same in its fundamentals: lobsters, salmon, roast beef, roast chicken, game *pâté*, tongue, *'sandwiches variés'*, chocolate éclaires. The presence of champagne was taken for granted.

But even Ascot was only a preparation for the event that marked the climax of the picnicker's year: Henley. For all but the specialists who were actually interested in the rowing, Henley was *the* picnic of the Season: a three-day *fête champêtre*, held both by and on the water. At Henley there was room to spread; room to serve and eat super-picnics that, while still consisting of the staple picnic fodder of lobster, tongue, game and cake, ran into ten courses or more; room, in the floating townships Society set up for itself, to store whole cellars of champagne. Even people who made do with the most basic type of picnic, involving merely a tablecloth, a rug, a shady tree and grass, still ate in style: 'What hampers,' says an 1897 *Lady* with feeling,

> are drawn out from under coach-boxes and waggonette seats, with their ice pails swathed in flannels, and bottles of soda water, the lemons and claret. And what marvellous pies are cut, and impromptu salads compounded! And how the hawkers wind in and out among the picnic parties, with their baskets of late strawberries, and first ripe gooseberries, and cherries, and bananas galore!

After this high spot, a slow but definite decline set in that ended in the austere autumn picnics of the serious sportsman, working singly or in small parties. At rock bottom, these were plain affairs of game pie, cold beef and a hip flask; a further item—trout fried on an open fire—depended on the morning's progress in the river.

For most male members of the upper classes, and for many of those members of the upper-middle class who could afford it, sport was an all-year-round business, just like the various forms of picnics that accompanied it. In one or more of its different branches, sport was studied, practised or at least discussed with zeal in practically every Top Victorian and Edwardian household. With the noted exception of hunting (and, to some extent, of fishing), it was not particularly a ladies' affair: ladies attached to a shooting party, for instance, were expected to appear for lunch and then disappear again, or at least stay well out of the way. Indeed, the 'ladies' game' of the fully-developed Victorian Season was tacked on to a programme of summer events that had in most cases been well-established fixtures before the Victorian era had got under way. The oldest of them all was Ascot, inaugurated by Queen Anne in 1711; its Royal Procession was founded by the Prince Regent when he finally came to the throne as George IV. The Derby arrived in 1780, having overcome its 50–50 risk of being called the Bunbury instead. (The Earl of Derby had developed the idea in collaboration with a fellow enthusiast, Sir Charles Bunbury; when, over the dinner table, the question of naming the race arose, they simply tossed a coin to decide.) Goodwood was a turn-of-the-century introduction: the first public Goodwood race-meeting took place in 1802.

In a sense, Henley started in 1829. The first aquatic

contest held there, however, was in fact the first-ever Varsity Boat Race (Oxford won). Seven years were to elapse before the contestants met again—in London, this time—but memories of the bonanza business the race had brought them later helped the Henley authorities to make the momentous decision that, from 1839 onwards, a regatta of their own should become a permanent fixture. The first one was enlivened by continual volleys of pistol shots, church bells ringing from every tower, huge crowds and two bands. Only the umpire, the organisers appealed, should attempt to follow the races along the bank on horseback.

The other great organiser of aquatic contests, the Yacht Club at Cowes, had more aristocratic, and earlier, beginnings. In 1812, Georgian yachting enthusiasts banded together with two aims: 'to associate pleasure with profit, and to establish on a patriotic basis, a national and splendid festival, worthy of the brightest age of England'. Thirteen peers were present at the club's formal inauguration and, since part of the intention was to boost methods of naval construction generally, the club received both royal and government encouragement. When the Prince Regent— elected to membership in 1817—succeeded to the throne, the club got its 'Royal' prefix; when his brother, William IV, presented the club with a hundred guineas challenge cup, he also indicated that it should be called the Royal Yacht Squadron. Even Queen Victoria, who on the whole saw little point in sports, presented a cup when her turn came round.

Ascot, Henley, Goodwood, Cowes: these were the main sporting events that the leisured classes proceeded to incorporate into their ladies' festival of the Season. The Derby, in an indefinable way, never quite made the top Society stakes, and for a significant reason. In its double capacity as the most popular and the most important race of the year, it belonged to society with a small 's'. It was the nearest thing industrial England had to one of the great pre-industrial fairs. Society had no hope of excluding the gypsies, eel-sellers, acrobats, beggars and race-goers of every conceivable social class that it attracted, nor even of sizeably reducing their numbers. The fixture stubbornly retained the total social mix that had been a characteristic of the eighteenth-century sporting gathering, patronised by Royalty and ragamuffins alike. When, in 1896, the Prince of Wales's horse Persimmon followed the example set over a hundred years before by Sir Thomas, owned by Prinny, and won the two and a half minute race, Edward's success was cheered by a representative cross-section of the entire British people.

Ascot, however, was rather different, as were the other major sporting events of the social calendar's London Season. Ascot had both its formally-stated Royal connections and, in its Royal Enclosure, a real-life version of the upper classes' protective palisade. Goodwood's protection was its distance from London; the meeting took added lustre from its ducal patronage. Henley also had its enclosures in the shape of its rowing-club lawns, entry to which was applied for well in advance (houseboat parties joined a separate queue, for river space). The Royal Yacht Squadron—strictly speaking, Cowes was a post-Season fixture but had earned its place as a glittering appendage to it—had exclusivity built into its very rules: new members were only admitted if they owned a vessel of over ten tons and had received not more than one black ball out of a possible ten in the ballot to decide their membership.

Once rendered as exclusive as rules, distance and iron railings could make them, all four gatherings could be used for the Season's normal purposes: as a setting for social intercourse, as a parade ground on which wealth could be displayed and as a specialised section of the marriage-market. Young men, as chagrined hostesses found time and time again, were not particularly keen dancers; they were usually, however, keen race-goers. And it was at events lasting several days rather than several hours that girls sizing up a *parti* could get the beginnings of an idea of his true temperament. Here, against a neatly-described Ascot background, is how two admirers of Grenville Murray's archetype show up.

It is then that the Flirt sees how ill the sportive young baronet bears his losses on the turf, while the middle-aged merchant, who has, perhaps, lost three times as much, remains as serene as ever. The one stands revealed as a cantankerous cub; the other as a man of nerve and good taste. Race succeeds race, and the differences become more accentuated. In the evening, at dinner, the baronet is absent-minded and sour, talks of the villainy of book-makers, and swears that his favourite was 'roped'; the merchant overflows with anecdote, and proves that his appetite has not been impaired a jot.

The next day, at luncheon, on the top of a drag which has been tooled down from London by some noble member of the Four-in-Hand Club [coach-driving was another highly exclusive sport] the young baronet drinks too much champagne, and his hand trembles as he holds up his field-glass to watch the start in a race on which he has risked a pot of money; the elderly merchant meanwhile devotes himself to the Flirt, and shows by his light chatting that he has an eye for something beyond the pecuniary aspects of a race. He points out the beauties of the course, the multicoloured line of jockeys breaking up for a preliminary canter, the picturesque effect of the mass of carriages thronging near the stand. Nor does he forget to make an appointment to meet his fair companion again at Goodwood.

Into the well-spaced timetable of the Season's major sporting events, others, such as Society's two formal visits to Lord's—for the Varsity and the Eton and Harrow matches—fitted with ease. For Britain's leaders, indeed, the Eton and Harrow (with, of course, its attendant picnic) was a cross between an Old Boy's Reunion and a Parent's Day: for Society in general, however, the match was a mere pretext for seeing and being seen. As a *Country Life* ladies' columnist—a petulant and presumably fictional featherhead writing under the name of Mlle Sans-Gêne—commented in the late 1890s, 'how much more tolerable these functions at Lord's would be without the cricket'. (To do her justice, Mademoiselle is invaluable to twentieth-century researchers, not just for what she says, but for the idea she gives of what, in her public's view, a Society lady was expected to be. And she does have her moments: 'I remain down in the country,' she notes in an early September issue, 'getting fat on grouse and idleness.') Eton's Fourth of June—held on the birthday of King George III, to commemorate a visit he paid to the college—fell into much the same pattern. Old Etonians revisited their youth; parents of young ones listened to the speeches, watched the cricket match, the procession of boats and the fireworks. The event had a useful by-product in that it allowed daughters not yet 'out' to be seen and appraised; a more curious thread was woven into the affair when, in the

years between the First and Second World Wars, divorce
became a more commonplace fact of life among the upper
class. In the cases where a boy had one-and-a-half sets of
parents, or even two whole ones, his real father and mother
would join forces for the day with poise and amity.

The London Season contained one further sporting event:
a continual one, that took place every day except Sunday
and received active and ardent support from both men and
women. They rode. First thing in the morning, they headed
towards Hyde Park's Rotten Row and cantered up and down
for exercise, for enjoyment and—it is more than likely—for
sheer release of the emotions that, under the rules by which
they lived, were kept tightly under control. Hippolyte Taine
did not, on the whole, care for the way English women
looked (he found their 'long projecting teeth' particularly
distressing), but he made an exception for those early-risers
in the Park.

> Many of the horsewomen are charming, so simple, and so
> serious, without a trace of coquetry; they come here not to
> be seen, but to take the air; their manner is frank without
> pretension; their shake of the hand quite loyal, almost
> masculine; no frippery in their attire; the small black vest,
> tightened at the waist, moulds a fine shape and healthy
> form; to my mind, the first duty of a young lady is to be in
> good health. They manage their horses with complete
> ease and assurance.

Their skill was not surprising. Most of them would have
been learning to manage their horse since childhood, and,
Season notwithstanding, the lives of the really keen
horsewomen centred round one single date: 1 November,
the start of hunting.

Given its firm place in the Olde Englande myth,
hunting—fox-hunting—started surprisingly late. Until
sometime in the middle of the eighteenth century, the stag
held pride of place in huntsmen's thoughts. The hare was
also a top-ranking form of game; two more, the wild boar
and the wolf, had given up the furious but finally unequal
struggle in the seventeenth century. The fox was considered
as vermin—although a form of vermin that could certainly
run fast. However, the disappearance of British forests and
the eighteenth-century enclosure of land brought drastic

changes to the hunting scene. The stag was steadily driven back to its ultimate fastnesses in Exmoor, the New Forest and Scotland (where the practice of stalking rather than hunting the animal grew up in the nineteenth century); the hare—which, like the deer, was hunted on horseback in the eighteenth century—had a brief period as Top Beast. But, here and there, country landowners were getting up at four in the morning and jogging off with their hounds to take part in a rather slow, rather sedate chase after the one-time mere nuisance. By degrees, the new sport spread, as did the idea of speed: it was no longer thought flashy to gallop or to take fences on the run rather than from a standstill. And, by the end of the eighteenth century, fox-hunting was well on the way to collecting the near-national support, the assortment of notable eccentrics and the extraordinarily large body of legend, tradition and literary references that it soon possessed.

That it was an upper-class sport—or, at least, that it was led and controlled by the upper class—was inevitable. All questions of expenditure apart, it was extremely time-consuming. Naturally, the question of what was and was not 'done' occurred again and again: true huntsmen were not merely members of their own specialist club but of the much more important one of the country's élite. Thus, it was not done to say that one 'went out hunting'; one 'hunted'. It was not done, as Lady Colin Campbell reminded her readers, to hunt in pink unless one was 'a regular member of some hunt and is a *bona fide* hunting man, who means to ride straight across country'. The vocabulary involved was enormous: babbler, billett, break and break up; draft, drag, draw; head and headed and heads up; kennel, music, mute . . . . And the number of mistakes a newcomer could make was equally huge.

A simple lack of courage was one of the more obvious ones: 'nervous or unskilful horsemen are continuously jeered at,' comments Taine, having skimmed through three volumes of *Punch* and noted the predominance of hunting humour; 'jokes are cracked about distinguished foreigners who shrink from a leap, or who fear to break their necks.' By contrast, the equestriennes to whose fascination he constantly falls victim 'leap hedges, ditches, five-barred gates, dash through the underwood, gallop over the marshes, and come in at the finish with a rush, carrying their horses over every obstacle, putting inexperienced fox-hunters to the blush'.

Even more pronounced, though, was the quantity of cheerfully heartless humour expended on the outsider: the novice, the bumbler or the social climber of either sex. That women frequently employed this unreliable route towards higher social status is shown by a stern passage in a *Country Life* analysis of huntswomen one could do without; one type 'generally uses the hunting field as a means of climbing into a society that otherwise she would never be seen in. She has heard the hunting field called a leveller of class, and she is determined to take advantage of it . . . she has no nerve, and no love of hounds or horses.' Beside her, the article's other targets—the pretty show-offs, the chatterboxes and the nervous ones who hunt on doctor's orders—are let down with the most harmless of mockery.

True keenness, however, made up for lack of gentility. The greatest hunting hero in Victorian fiction is no member of the aristocracy but Surtees' Jorrocks, a Cockney merchant whose view on hunting is, 'By 'eavens, it's sublime!' None of the other field sports—not even the Victorians' own refinement, shooting on a gigantic and scientifically-organised scale—produced anything that quite matched him. 'Scientific' was, of course, the Victorians' own way of regarding the practical back-up that shooting in their period received—which, in its fashion, it was; the industry was supported by gunsmiths, gamekeepers, beaters and the owners of uncomfortable but strategically-placed country houses and in its turn supported commercial purveyors of game. To us, however, there seems little that is scientific in spirit about the hopes expressed, say, by one 'Rockwood', a sporting writer of the 1880s, who proclaimed himself 'determined to have fair good sport at everything that rose, from a jack snipe to a barnacle goose'. To the present writer, at least, there is also something depressingly obsessive about the photographed sportsmen flanked by positive carpets of pheasants and something incomprehensible about the sentimentality with which they drenched their pleasure. The ptarmigan, 'Rockwood' goes on in a spurt of lyricism,

in summer lives joyously in the sunshine light of early and late sun-rise; in winter, amongst the snow, it passes its time cheerfully under the blankets of mist, or sits sheltered in a crevice when the fierce gales sweep across the summit in all their fury . . . . Wrapping up the lovely-plumaged little things, whose white feathers were stained with little scarlet drops, we struck across a flat piece of the hill, in order to catch them at another point.

Artless musings on Nature, however, were only part of the shooting picture. Far more on the sportsman's mind were the eternal questions of cost, equipment and logistics. A grouse enthusiast journeying north in August, for example, needed the following accessories, either in the luggage van behind him or awaiting him on the spot: guns and cartridges; dogs; a keeper who knew his business; means of on-site transport; servants; habitation that was reasonably warm, reasonably dry and equipped with reasonable drainage (many Highland shooting lodges tended to deficiency in all three respects); shooting rights over the patch of ground involved; several changes of clothes; and ready money. Money was important, since a complicated system of tipping prevailed; that it was also a lavish system is indicated by the Langley Moores in what, for the upper classes, was the slightly less well-heeled inter-war period. 'At a large highly-organised shoot,' they explain,

> each 'gun' will give the head keeper not less than a pound and add, perhaps, half-a-crown or five shillings for any man who has done him an individual service: even at much smaller gatherings, the keeper's tip will be ten shillings. Big shoots lasting several days cost every member easily a pound in tips, apart from what may be given to indoor staff.

On the whole, a *nouveau riche* anxious to win acceptance from the shooting fraternity had a rather better chance of success than his opposite number who hunted. For one thing, the rules of the sport were less arcane: any uncertain sportsman could discover the opening and closing dates for each gamebird's season in an almanac, while the most crucial rule of all had even found its way into easily-remembered rhyme:

> All the pheasants ever bred
> Won't repay for one man dead.

More important, it was often only a *nouveau riche* who could lay on the carpet-of-pheasant effect in which the later

Victorians and their successors delighted. By the last quarter
of the nineteenth century, the finances of the landed upper
class were beginning to tremble before the onslaught of an
agricultural depression; the 'new money' of the rich
industrialists at last had a chance to provide them with a sure
passport to social success.

Hunting did, though, give the rules of Society a small jolt
in another way. Taine was not alone in admiring a
well-turned-out horsewoman; the hunting field was, in fact,
the only place where a Victorian lady could compete directly
with men at their own game and, in addition, not be thought
unfeminine if she won. Men might be in slight awe of a
'regular Diana', but they would also admire her: admire her
to the point of paying court. As might be expected, hunting
flirtations were common, the hunting love-story a recognised
literary variant on the main theme.

Moreover, the huntswoman in search of a husband had
one huge advantage over her stay-at-home sister; she could
not, for obvious reasons, be chaperoned. It was a straw that
showed the way the wind blew. As developments of the late
nineteenth century were to prove, freedom from
authority—both the authority of the family and the overall
authority exercised by upper-class Society as a
whole—depended to a surprisingly large extent on how fast
members of that family and Society could move physically.
From this simple fact, demonstrated at the height of the
social rule-book's power over those who followed its
sub-section on the hunting field, would emerge some
remarkable developments.

Archery in Regent's Park, 1894

∞∞

CHAPTER TWELVE

Country Houses

> As if to demonstrate their three great traditional talents—for playing politics, for accumulating wealth, and for designing lovely landscapes—the English work best at the first two against a background developed by the third. For generations most of what has happened to mortals and money in London, and often what has happened to Europe, has first been planned in the talk of prominent Englishmen weekending with a purpose among the green trees and fields of some beautiful bucolic shire.
>
> Janet Flanner, writing in the
> *New Yorker*, 1938

In the 1890s, a new toy hit the British leisured classes and went off like a bomb. It was the bicycle, much improved by Mr Dunlop's pneumatic tyre. As Gwen Raverat notes in *Period Piece*, 'bicycling became the smart thing in Society, and the lords and ladies had their pictures in the papers, riding along in the park, in straw boater hats.' The young Gwen herself was promoted to wearing real knickerbockers under her cycling frock and over her frilly drawers; further mannish—and therefore 'liberated'—accessories worn by ladies at the time were the tweed jacket, shirt and tie pioneered by that former disgrace to her sex, the New Woman.

In finery like this, *Country Life's* Mlle Sans-Gêne pedalled off to the Park—Regent's Park in this case, although Hyde Park was normally the regular cycling venue—and there, unencumbered by chaperon or rules, actually *met a man*. Their described (and probably invented) encounter was innocence itself: Randolph smoked a cigarette and 'talked with contempt of culture', while Mademoiselle admired the view. But its implications were obvious. Not only could a fashionable unmarried girl proclaim this remarkable new access of independence, but she could do so without transgressing the rules to any great extent. For the rules themselves were changing.

Within a matter of months rather than years, they were to change still further. They had been developed to service a group whose members, to a greater or lesser degree, were all acquainted with each other and who, at appointed moments, were in the habit of collecting in the same place and staying there for an appreciable length of time. The arrival of the horseless carriage would help to break this system into pieces. The upper classes suddenly found that there were pursuits just as prestigious, and far more amusing, than driving sedately in the Park behind a pair of bulging, tail-switching rumps. One go-ahead spirit after another leapt at the chance of careering round the country at 18 mph, frightening horses and lady cyclists (who tended to fall off in panic), being jeered at by cabbies and Oldest Inhabitants, taking pot-shots at rabbits mesmerised by the acetylene lamps, double-declutching at every gear change, and broadening his—or her—experience of life in all directions. An early (1902) motorist wrote happily of the way the new sport extended 'in delightful manner' the range of the participants' personal friendships and promoted pleasant social intercourse of both sexes. It did—and it would continue to do so. Against the charm, convenience and fascinating intricacy of motoring, the rules laid down by the dowagers of times past seemed more faded than ever, while the social calendar the dowagers and their husbands had refined would never be quite the same again.

The automobile first began to attract its British public in 1896, when the first of all our motor shows—held at the Crystal Palace—was followed by the repealing of the 1861 Act that insisted that a self-propelled vehicle on the road should be heralded by a man walking in front with a red flag. (He could easily keep ahead of his charge: the Act also stated that no self-propelled vehicle might travel at more than 4 mph.) Within four years, complaints were thronging in about outrageous 'scorching' on the highways. Lord Carnarvon, a noted offender, roared along at 24 mph, his Jehu's progress throwing up towering clouds of dust and attracting the increasingly blasé attentions of the police. Another noble enthusiast was the highest-ranking man in the whole country: Edward VII took to cars with delight and commuted between Marlborough House and Windsor 'as fast', according to one commentator, 'as it is done by train'. All the cars he owned were painted a distinctive claret red, and any occupiers of the road who spotted a red car scorching up behind them did well to draw in and await events. The King believed in having the road clear ahead of him as far as he could see, and offending vehicles were ruthlessly caught up and overtaken. As to speed, Lord Carnarvon's efforts were quickly put in the shade: in 1906 the King and his chauffeur set a record themselves by managing 60 mph on the London to Brighton road.

It would take time before the automobile's profound effects on society as a whole would be felt, but one drew itself to attention almost instantly. In the late 1890s, Hyde Park's Church Parade was still as crowded with the rich, the beautiful and the important as it had ever been. By 1909, it was not only possible to see the grass between the people but to wonder at its ever having been invisible. There were fewer carriages to be seen there on Saturdays, fewer social fixtures altogether; Sunday afternoons at the Botanical Gardens or the Zoo became almost a memory. London, helped by the horseless carriage, emptied on those two days, for Society had discovered the week-end. In the Edwardian period, the Upper Ten Thousand varied their normal migratory flow of London/abroad/country by breaking up the London part of it into a jerkier rhythm of Town/country/Town, to be repeated as long as the supply of invitations held out. As far as the automobile and the railway could between them reach, dowagers, aristocrats, social lions of the day, useful young men and Society women were re-discovering the amenities of the English country house.

'Re-discovering', because the vast bulk of the upper classes had country houses of their own. The country was the place where they had grown up to school or coming-out age; where, except for the most determined travellers, they still spent a great part of each year; where carefully-selected friends came on visits that could last into weeks. For the heads of families, the country provided a business, a sportsground and a considerable (though fluctuating) income. For late-arrivers in Society, the ownership of land and a house to go with it were indispensable accessories to the business of keeping up with the crowd. For women, the country was simply the place—pleasing or tedious, according to taste—where one lived. The country was where English Society came from.

If the members of that Society knew all about the country, they also knew—if by hearsay only—all that was to be known about country houses. They were well aware that these varied in character from the modest to the grandiose; from the comfortable to the bleak (all authorities agree, however, in pointing out that even a comfortable country house was incredibly cold); from the cosily Philistine to the downright eerie. In the last category, Glamis probably headed the list: as the well-known story goes, a lively house-party there once decided to track down the family secret by hanging a towel at every window that could be found and thus—from the lawn—spotting the hidden room where the alleged mystery was concealed. They spotted not one unadorned window but three; but, before they could investigate further, they were sent packing in disgrace. A chill of a different order is provided by Taine, who reports the Marquess of Hertford. 'I have a mansion in Wales', the Marquess had said,

> which I have never seen, but which I am told is very fine. Every day dinner for twelve is served there, and the carriage drawn up at the door in case I should arrive. The butler eats the dinner. Go thither, make yourself at home; you see that it will not cost you a farthing.

Admittedly, this invitation dates back to the mid-nineteenth century, when railways were only beginning to reach beyond the main towns; but an even more striking picture of lonely grandeur is provided by the retiring Duke of Portland, who reigned over Welbeck Abbey from 1854 to 1879. The Duke, a tremendous builder, constructed the following during his term of ownership: a mile-long underground carriage tunnel, lit by skylights and gas jets, from his coach-house to the edge of his estates; a windowless riding school (the second largest in the world), also lit by gas; a quarter-mile indoor gallop; an underground conservatory with a glass roof; and a huge subterranean ballroom, 174 feet long. But no balls were held there; not because visitors could not reach Welbeck Abbey (the Duke used to travel up to London by train himself, inside a shuttered coach loaded on a truck), but because their host was too shy to receive them if they came. Like the mad King Ludwig of Bavaria, the Duke's aim was to build himself a palace more suited to fantasy than real life and then to hide himself in the middle of it.

At the time that this pathetic aristocrat was ordering all his tunnelling operations, Taine was making a study of some more representative types of English country house. The grandest of his examples is a domain of seven hundred acres.

> The house is a large mansion, rather commonplace, solid in appearance, arranged in modern style; the furniture of the ground floor and of the first floor, recently renewed, cost four thousand pounds. Three rooms or drawing-rooms, sixty feet long, twenty high, are furnished with large mirrors, good pictures, excellent engravings, with bookcases. In front is a glazed conservatory, where one passes the afternoon when the weather is bad, and where, even in winter, one can fancy that it is spring.

He did not find the decorations to his taste, though he did approve of two other things: the atmosphere of spaciousness and his own bedroom. This, he points out with delight, was carpeted throughout, except for the oilcloth by the wash-stand; it had two dressing-tables, four different sorts of towel and three pairs of candles; and 'another indispensable cabinet in the room is a marvel.'

He goes on:

> The servant comes four times a day into the room; in the morning to draw the blinds and the curtains, open the inner blinds, carry off the boots and clothes, bring a large can of hot water with a fluffy towel on which to place the feet; at midday, and at seven in the evening, to bring water and the rest, in order that the visitor may wash before luncheon and dinner; and at night to shut the window, arrange the bed, get the bath ready, renew the linen; all this with silence, gravity, and respect. Pardon these trifling details; but they must be handled in order to figure to oneself the wants of any Englishman in the direction of his luxury; what he expends in being waited upon and comfort is enormous, and one may laughingly say that he spends the fifth of his life in his tub.

This, tub and all, was what the Edwardian country house owner inherited from his Victorian parents. He would proceed to put in bathrooms (always hotly scrimmaged for by guests), he would increase the atmosphere of plushness and he would cover the Victorian brown paint with lots of glossy white. But the fundamentals would remain unchanged. Silence, gravity and respect would continue to be the ideal characteristics of a servant; the English gentleman's notion of an ideal way of life would still include fluffy towels, clean linen and hot water. And a new guest wing, built in that distinctive Edwardian style with its faint connotations of the seaside, would still be 'rather commonplace', solid in appearance and equipped with the latest comforts in bedroom furniture. To sum up, the owner and his wife—particularly his wife—planned to welcome their guests to an establishment that had much in common with a good hotel.

Indeed, to all intents and purposes it *was* a hotel: a hotel where all the residents had been introduced. The more leisurely style of country house party, lasting a week or more, had an atmosphere more like that of a club, in that the guest's personalities, talents, quirks had time to emerge and be accepted (relatives, of course, might visit for anything up to a lifetime). In addition, many of the visitors were actively devoted to some purpose other than mere visiting. 'There's a good bit of rough shooting,' a host would say; and his guest would accept the invitation with alacrity. But the weekend, with its jittery Saturday-to-Monday feeling, offered an atmosphere more like that of an extremely luxurious caravanserai: there was no time to get set into anything before the moment came to be off.

From the hostess's point of view, it was a concentrated demonstration of all her social capabilities, more difficult—because longer—even than a dinner party. From the standpoint of her guests, it was a proof both of their social capabilities and of their social standing. To make sure of the latter point, lists of who was at who's were printed in the *Morning Post* every Monday: it was see and be seen all over again, with the newspaper ensuring a good large audience. And only two types of raw material were needed to achieve this symbolic triumph; people (as many as possible) and the money to ensure that the background equipment —the servants, the food, the transport—all ran as smoothly as clockwork; as, in fact, it does in a hotel.

For any guests so unworldly as to be unsure of playing

their own part in the weekend ritual, Lady Colin Campbell
had some useful information to give. She deals, in the main,
with the two vexed questions of outstaying one's welcome
and tipping. 'A lady', *Good Society* points out

> gives to the maid who has assisted her with her toilet, and
> the housemaid. A gentleman remembers the valet, butler,
> coachman, game-keeper—any and all who have rendered
> him any service, and the donations are according to the
> wealth of the donor; but as a rule, the men-servants in
> *large* houses expect gold.

Gold would certainly have been expected in a country
house as prestigious as the one acidly described by Harold
Nicolson in *Small Talk*, and a guest ignorant of these niceties
would scarcely have been present. In his unloving portrait of
the Edwardian weekend, Mr Nicolson starts a typical Sunday
off with one of those vast breakfasts. From then on, the
schedule was as follows: church; an uneasy pre-lunch pause,
during which the women refurbished themselves; lunch
itself, with orchids on the table and general conversation.
Then came a period of free time: time for a stroll in the park,
time for a drive to Stonehenge, time for a sleep. After that,
there was tea, with scones, cucumber sandwiches, cake,
Tiptree jam, and lobster salad if the King came.

The gap between tea and dinner (at 8.30) was filled by
billiards for the men and the invaluable bridge. Bridge tables
were laid out in the red drawing-room. The women relied on
an hour's grace for changing into dinner dresses and
reconvened slowly in the yellow saloon, showing off their
clothes. 'Then there would be dinner. Ptarmigan and
champagne. Champagne and ptarmigan . . . .'

After dinner—which the ladies left at 9.45; the men joined
them at 10.15—there was more bridge; and, at midnight,
those still hungry ate devilled chicken and sandwiches and
finally went to bed. 'I do not regret', Mr Nicolson
concluded,

> that I was old enough to touch the fringe of Edwardian
> luxury. But I render thanks to Providence that I was also
> young enough to relish and share the wider liberties of
> our subsequent age. Let us be frank about it. The
> Edwardians were vulgar to a degree . . . their intricacies
> were expensive but futile.

His wife, Vita Sackville-West, adds a further point in her own book on the Edwardians. The house party at the ducal mansion has started to talk politics, under the observing eye of explorer, social 'lion' and disaffected guest Leonard Anquetil.

These ladies and gentlemen spoke with a proprietary and casual familiarity, somewhat as though politics were children that they entrusted to the care of nurses and tutors . . . but although they were careful to give an impression of being behind the scenes, like parents who go up to the nursery once a day, their acquaintance remained oddly remote and no more convincing than an admirably skilful bluff. It was founded, Anquetil discovered, on personal contact with politicians: 'Henry told me last week . . .' or 'A. J. B. was dining with me and said . . .' but their chief desire was to cap one another's information.

Society with its big S had moved a considerable distance in the half century since one of the titled ladies of the time had been told, 'You ought to be a Prime Minister's wife; if you had been Lord John's [Lord John Russell] you would have kept the Whig party together.'

The lady thus addressed was Frances, Countess Waldegrave, daughter of a Jewish singer, widow of not one but two Waldegraves (to get round the deceased husband's brother's law, she and her second husband were married in Scotland) and one of the most powerful society hostesses of her day. Guests at her country houses—the most famous of which, Strawberry Hill, was in still-rural Twickenham—included Sir Robert Peel, Gladstone, the Duke of Newcastle and the Disraelis. It was Lady Waldegrave who helped rising politicians and social aspirants to realise the goals; it was her Twickenham house that provided a setting in which the innermost ring of the political world could function. (There was one celebrated occasion, however, when her social skills proved useless: at the heart of a government crisis no less than four cabinet ministers were under her roof, and, in the words of one contemporary, they 'kept such a watch on one another that even Lady Waldegrave could get at nothing definite, except that we are to have no revelations till they have seen the Queen, who is at Windsor tomorrow'. The upshot was the resignation of Prime Minister Russell—

whose own unsophisticated wife had contributed to his difficulties by her lack of social success.)

Lady Waldegrave—half Jewish, of 'low' birth and one-time inhabitant of the less certain areas of respectability—was unique in character and abilities; in her career as political hostess she was not. The picture Trollope draws in his *Palliser* novels of political power exercised in Westminster, in London drawing-rooms and in a succession of country houses did no more than reflect reality. At that time, power still lay in great part with the owners of those country houses. For a host and his guests to discuss its use in one direction or another—while the hostess smiled, tactfully withdrew, or, if she were extremely gifted, joined in—was no more unusual than for two office colleagues of today to talk shop at a party. It was the pool they all swam in.

But, by the time the Edwardian weekenders came chattering on the scene, that pool had ebbed. They may not have noticed it, but they were in the process of being left high and dry. With successive Reform Acts, the political power the Top Victorians had enjoyed had shifted away from their hands into those of the middle classes. (The working class and all women would not be enfranchised until after the First World War.) The introduction of death duties in 1894 was an indication that the financial power that they also enjoyed was from now on to come under increasingly serious attack. Lloyd George's proposed revolutionary budget, that put forward measures like a super-tax and a tax on land values, was not far off, and his question whether the country was 'to be governed by the King and the Peers or by the King and the People' would warn even the most mossbacked among the aristocracy that the game was almost up.

And so it was, as far as the House of Lords itself was concerned. In 1911, an even more revolutionary bill that turned the Lords' power to veto measures into mere power to postpone them was finally hammered through. But, despite both this and the world war that supervened shortly afterwards, the Lords themselves and the upper classes with them managed to continue to live in the style to which they were accustomed. True, the combination of death duties and increased taxation led to much selling off of property after 1918; many of the great town houses were separated from the families whose names they bore (and in some cases pulled down), while the qualification for inclusion in

Burke's Landed Gentry fell from its pre-war mark of two thousand acres to three hundred in 1935. But the country-houses—along with the débutantes, the Season, the sports-man's calendar and a modified form of the upper-class rulebook—continued to survive.

At Woburn, each guest had a personal footman standing behind his chair at dinner; at the Portlands' Welbeck Abbey, efforts to make economies resulted, so a story runs, in no more than a decision to stop the supply of private sealing wax to each guest's bedroom. The Duke of Devonshire's family gatherings at Chatsworth—complete with visiting servants—ran to over a hundred people.

The Second World War made further drastic inroads on upper-class wealth and on the houses that represented a proportion of it. 'But', comments a modern authority on the aristocracy, 'a surprising number of the old mansions survive and still house the descendants of the nobility who built them.' Among these are the Dukes of Northumberland (Alnwick Castle), Norfolk (Arundel) and Rutland (Belvoir). Dropping down from the ranks of dukes to earls, the Earl of Pembroke is on post-war record as complaining that he could afford only a butler, footman, cook, two housemaids and some daily cleaners for his own Wilton House. Many other mansion-owners, meanwhile, have cheerfully gone into the stately home business, some of them adding lions, vintage cars or costumes worn in successful television series to their estates' attractions.

As an entity, then, the upper-class country house does not seem in the mood to lie down and die. Indeed, large weekend house parties in some measure still continue to take place, mainly centred—as might be expected—round sport. What, however, about the rest of the social calendar, as defined in the early part of this book? Has the whole complicated structure followed one of its main supports—the armies of servants—into oblivion? Or is it proving tough enough to withstand the economic conditions of the 1970s?

The answer defies most, if not all, expectations.

CHAPTER THIRTEEN

∽∽∽

Today

There's life in the old dog yet.

Anon

A débutante of the 1930s contemplates three different Seasons, pre-war, post-war and present. 'As far as I was concerned', she says,

> it was all done terribly simply—not at all in a deb sort of way. No balls or anything. I just happened to have relatives living in London, so I went to be presented with my aunt and my mother. You didn't have to wear white any longer—I had a dress of pale pink—but it was still very grand: when you arrived at Buckingham Palace, there were all sorts of things you weren't used to, like footmen; even Beefeaters, I think.
> It took place in the evening, at six-thirty or so—we'd sat in the Mall for hours in the chauffeur-driven car we'd borrowed—and afterwards there was a tremendously grand buffet supper; yes, there was gold plate, and the orchestra played things from Gilbert and Sullivan. Frightening? No, not really; you just didn't want to fall over when you made your curtsey, or catch your heel in your hem. And you knew plenty of people there, a lot of your school friends and so on. And the fact that you'd been to Court meant you could go into the Royal Enclosure at Ascot, which was very nice, and to a Royal garden party—it was all just a very nice way of meeting people.

After the war, she presented her own daughter. By this time, some changes had taken place.

> The Court was in the afternoon, so you didn't get supper afterwards; it was tea and little cakes. And the clothes were quite different. No train, no feathers: we wore afternoon dresses and hats, little '50s hats on the back of

the head. And my daughter was just about to start training as a nurse, so she wasn't a very debby deb either.

And now? Well, it really has changed now, I think. In my day, things didn't *have* to be terribly expensive. All you needed was a dress to wear and someone to take you—that's all that was wanted for my presentation, since someone had lent us the car. I had a twenty-first dance in London, at the Mayfair Hotel, but I don't think that cost a very great deal either. I just can't imagine, though, what the bill for that would be nowadays.

You really need money now: if you've got it, you can do all these things—give dances in hotels, go to Ascot and so on—but a lot of them are now way beyond what middle-class people can afford. And besides, attitudes have changed: I very much enjoyed my time as a deb, but now you'd probably feel it was an absolute waste of time and money even to buy a special dress. I'd say there probably isn't a Society scene any more; heavens, we're all working people now, anyway.

The startling thing about this account is that practically every detail of the '30s deb's own passage into adulthood is now a matter for memory only (Ascot and the garden parties are, of course, the exceptions). She herself, in company with her daughter, saw the beginnings of this slide into extinction: the change from long presentation dresses to short, the jettisoning of the Prince of Wales feathers, the arrival of the 'working deb'. The end of the presentation road was finally reached in 1958, when the Palace decided to drop the event.

Turning to dances, the Mayfair, far from quoting an astronomical figure for a twenty-first, now can't quote a price at all. 'We haven't had a ballroom for a long time,' the hotel explains. 'It's now a casino. Sixty people is our limit: we do have a few dinner-dances for that number, but it's usually firms having a Christmas party.' The Dorchester, also a great centre for dances in the inter-war period, still does them; but not for debs. 'Nobody', says a Dorchester spokesman,

gives coming-out dances any more. The last one we had was . . . oh, three or four years ago, at least. It's just gone by the board—people don't have the money to spend these days. I honestly don't think you'll find any of the

London hotels doing that sort of thing: people wanting to give a dance usually do it in the country now, in their home or someone else's. Besides, if you have a country house, and your neighbours all bring over their house parties, all your guests can be fed before they come—which helps cut down costs still further.

At the time of writing (early 1977), the costs of throwing a grand party are indeed formidable. The Dorchester's prices for a dinner-dance start at the rock-bottom minimum of £6·50 to £7·50 a head—'our normal price for a four-course dinner'—and do not take incidentals into account. A party given privately can save considerably on the drinks bill—'you could bring it down to half what you'd pay in a hotel,' says one expert—but then faces the equally essential question of supplying a roof over the dancers' heads. If your ball is to be on too grand a scale to fit into a house, you have to hire a marquee: the figures involved in this transaction can run as high as £4000.

Music is also a potential big spender: while a group badly needing a break can be got for as little as £30, a party-giver determined to make a splash by hiring a nationally-famed equivalent can find himself shelling out £500 or more—and that for only part of the evening. The gaps while the maestros rest are filled by less acclaimed performers at a cost of something like £150 for the evening. Discos, at an average cost of £80, are cheaper—but this fact, unfortunately, is too well known for complete comfort.

Nor are the party-goers, as opposed to the party-givers, exempt from expenditure. The '30s deb's requirements—a new dress and someone to go with—are still in force, but the sums paid out for the one and by the other are now harder to find. It was considerations such as these that, for 1977 at least, put a halt to one of the premier events of the débutante season, the Queen Charlotte's Ball. (It's at this that debs curtsey to a cake—or, more exactly, to the person who cuts it.) The tickets for the Queen Charlotte's, the proceeds from which go to Queen Charlotte's Maternity Hospital and the Chelsea Hospital for Women, represented the least of a guest's worries: ticket costs were no more than £8 for the ball and dinner, £3·50 for the ball only, and the organisers had of late made the after-dinner tickets their main selling target. But to no avail. 'Last year', the ball's president, Sylvia Darley, told the *Sunday Telegraph* in February 1977, 'it was so difficult to get the number of guests up to 800. And this year there are only about 60 debs.'

Sixty debs, compared with the annual three hundred or so who in palmier days curtseyed not to a cake but to their Sovereign in Buckingham Palace; country-house dances at which guests arrive with prudently-filled stomachs; the 'Society scene' which no longer exists . . . it all has that change-and-decay feeling which drifts around any manifestation of nineteenth-century ambition which is studied in its late-twentieth-century form. In this particular case, indeed, one could hardly expect otherwise. The intricate social calendar of the Victorians and Edwardians, depending as it did on wealth, leisure and regiments of hired hands, is by all the rules an even more likely candidate for change and decay than such perished concepts as British supremacy or the gold standard. But there are two things about this particular legacy from the past that make it a very peculiar one.

The first is that the calendar itself is still there: not vestigially so, but in what on paper at least looks like all its former glory. Each of the main public fixtures attended by the upper classes in the year of Queen Victoria's Diamond Jubilee is on the schedule for the Jubilee Year of her great-great-granddaughter. The big race meetings are still on: Epsom, Royal Ascot, Goodwood. There's the Eton and Harrow match at Lord's and the Regatta at Cowes. The Royal Academy opens its summer exhibition on 21 May; Henley starts on the last day of June. Eton's Fourth is, of course, fixed for ever. There is a special gala jubilee performance at Covent Garden; there is polo at a variety of centres. Wimbledon has moved from its provisional place on the Season's list into a permanent one; an inter-war arrival, Glyndebourne, is also now a firm fixture and gives enduring proof of the fact that opera always was Society's first love among the arts. There are several Royal garden parties, a considerable number of charity balls (the gap left by the Queen Charlotte's notwithstanding), a lot of concerts. Even the traditional Victorian move north of the border finds a parallel: the International Edinburgh Festival takes place in late August and early September and coincides with the Royal Highland Gathering at Braemar.

The heart of the social programme, then, has not only

survived practically intact but has even collected some additions. And the fact of its survival leads one on to the second extraordinary thing about the whole phenomenon. This is that, despite two world wars, both followed by major economic crises, and despite the sweeping changes in social attitudes that have accompanied Britain's move into the post-1945 era, the change and decay of the social calendar did not set in *at all* until this decade. Naturally, it has so far only made itself felt in the points where the support—and especially the financial support—for the programme was potentially weakest: its private events. The demise, temporary though the organisers hope it will be, of the Queen Charlotte's may be the first sign of something more serious.

It seems unbelievable—and the upper classes of the immediate post-war period would certainly not have believed it—but the fortunes of the upper-class social calendar and those who followed it actually soared during the 1960s to a point where they began to approach heights undreamt-of for over thirty years. 'By 1967', says Roy Perrott in *The Aristocrats*,

> there were at least six times more private events than there had been in the 1930s: about two hundred private dances in town and country, each with around four hundred guests, and a similar number of smaller ones; and five hundred cocktail parties. Though the number of 'official' debs had stayed about the same at four hundred, there were now reckoned to be at least 1,500 extra describing themselves as such. Competition for a mention in the gossip-columns had become fierce; public relations men were hired by some.

There was only one snag: to take part in proceedings to the limits of this new scale, you had to be rich; very rich indeed. For a short and glossy period, Britain's upper classes lived through the pre-Edwardian period all over again; the aristocracy provided the tone, wealthy businessmen provided the cash, and those who found themselves outranked on both fronts wondered sadly just how people could afford to keep in the swim.

But, although it was now considerably easier to infiltrate the bastions of Society, the old principle of upper-class solidarity still held good. As soon as anything looked like getting too popular, Society carefully slid away from it, leaving the aspirants high and dry. If it became too easy to dress in style, the true member of the upper classes would make a point of turning out in the most unassuming gear possible. Roy Perrott, researching in the late 1960s, was told that 'simply *no one* goes to the Eton and Harrow match these days, and one wouldn't be seen dead at *Henlah*.' Fashionable London restaurants included some modest establishments that, Formica tops and all, were at a quite astonishing remove from the traditional glories of the Ritz.

Everything seemed set for another Edwardian-style climax of entertainment and opulence when the 1973 oil crisis smashed it flat, along with a great deal else besides. Very quickly, the habit of exclusivity brought about its own destruction: party-givers realised that they could no longer afford to keep one jump ahead of their neighbours and quietly stopped trying altogether. According to inside accounts, it appears that even those who still had money to spare suddenly felt squeamish about its conspicuous consumption. The Americans, traditionally great injectors of foreign wealth into Britain's social calendar, were as affected as anyone by the state of affairs. The sheikhs moved in to London; the coming-out dance became all but a thing of the past; and, as this book was being written, the Queen Charlotte's Ball was cancelled. It looked as if the social scene really was at last going to join the gold standard, the Empire and the one-tier postal system as something that Britain could no longer afford to keep up. The account was obviously being closed, with an invisible line drawn underneath it. End of an era; end of a whole society with a small s; end of an extraordinary pattern of living whose main fault lay in its flagrant contrast with the overall social conditions prevailing when it was at its height and whose main virtue was the example of ordered excellence that at its best it provided.

Having researched up to this point, the writer felt that that was surely it. All that remained was to compose a suitable obituary. So what follows is in the nature of Stop Press: a single report from the hinterland, arriving seconds before the deadline, and presented here just as it stands. It comes from one of London's party-organising firms, Party Planners.

From 1973 to 1976, the social barometer represented by

the firm's order books showed a long, steep drop as far as the scale of privately-given parties was concerned. The lavish affairs of the 1960s seemed to have vanished from the aspirations of all involved. At the beginning of 1977, however, there were faint signs that the market was moving again, and by March those signs had turned themselves into hard-and-fast actuality. The coming-out dance is not dead; some will be taking place as this book is being printed. People will be going to balls. The dense wedge of the Season's public events—events that, thanks to the strength of tradition behind them, have so far withstood the ravages of the economic storm—will again be accompanied by their privately-given equivalents. 'I am terribly surprised and rather bewildered; I can't quite believe it,' says the firm's owner, Lady Elizabeth Anson. 'But it seems to be happening. In December, though, I'd have said the reverse.'

A straw in the wind—or the swallow that doesn't make a summer? The motivation behind this upsurge of interest is extremely obscure: it could be anything from Jubilee Year enthusiasm to sheer boredom at counting pennies. A certain caution with money is still evident, however; forced flowers are being replaced with hedgerow arrangements of daisies and cornstalks, while lobster, after a very long innings, seems to be disappearing from ballroom menus for ever. 'I think people are going back to what they really want to have themselves rather than what they think they ought to have,' Lady Elizabeth goes on. If a party-giver wants to serve sausages and mash, that's fine; 'as long as it's in the right dishes, and it's hot.'

The survival of this revised form of major social gathering is arguably crucial to the survival of the social calendar as a whole. As the Victorians discovered, it is only within the walls of a private establishment that control over who enters a social group can be properly maintained. If the calendar's life is to be a developing one, rather than that of a fossilised exhibit left over from another age, its supporters have to retain that group sense of identity that this same calendar helped them to build up over the period we have been studying. And the key to this ability to know who and what you are is the personal introduction represented by the invitation card; a ticket that can be bought is by no means the same thing.

But will it survive? And, indeed, should it? In the writer's view—admittedly a controversial one—the two questions are linked: if the social calendar is strong enough to carry on somehow, it deserves to be allowed to, untroubled by more than the occasional (and occasionally richly-deserved) jeer. The next three or four years are clearly going to be critical: by the 1980s, we will be looking either at a cross that marked the spot or at a new lease of life for something that has shown itself as fundamentally whaleboned and tough as the Victorian women who did so much to develop it. On balance, one feels that the odds are in favour of the latter. The practice of proclaiming a group's identity by its concerted actions is not a prerogative of the upper classes; to most members of every single social group in Britain—whether based on pub, office, shopping centre, playground, street corner, university or trade union headquarters—it comes as naturally as breathing. There is no reason why the ballroom, or whatever symbol of Society takes its place, should be exempt from the workings of that most basic rule of all.

An accidental meeting, 1885

Bibliography

All Round Sport with Fish, Fur & Feather, T. Dykes ('Rockwood'), Messrs. Fores, 1887

Amazing Grace, E. S. Turner, Michael Joseph, 1975

The Aristocrats, Roy Perrott, Weidenfeld and Nicolson, 1968

Below Stairs, Margaret Powell, Peter Davies, 1968

The Best Circle's (Society, Etiquette & the Season), Leonore Davidoff, Croom Helm, 1973

Bred for the Purple (A History of the Monarchy & the Turf), Michael Seth-Smith, Leslie Frewin, 1969

Brideshead Revisited, Evelyn Waugh, Chapman & Hall, 1945

Close of an Era: 1887–1914, Percy Colson, Hutchinson, 1945

Consuming Passions, Philippa Pullar, Hamish Hamilton, 1970

Cook's Guide and Housekeeper's and Butler's Assistant, Charles Elmé Francatelli; Richard Bentley & Son, 1880

The Early Victorian Woman, Janet Dunbar, Harrap, 1953

Edwardian Promenade, James Laver, E. Hulton & Co, 1958

The Edwardians, V. Sackville-West, The Bodley Head, 1930

The English Aristocracy, Marion Yass, Wayland, 1974

English Social Differences, T. H. Pear, Allen & Unwin, 1955

Etiquette of Good Society, Lady Colin Campbell, Cassell, 1911 (revised edition)

Fifty Years: 1882–1932, By 27 contributors to *The Times*, Thornton Butterworth, 1932

Heads of the People, essay collection published by David Bryce, *c.* 1840

Historical Costumes of England 1066–1968, N. Bradfield, Harrap, 1970 (third edition)

Holidays, Sheila Gordon, Batsford, 1972

Homes Sweet Homes, Osbert Lancaster, Murray, 1939

Hons and Rebels, Jessica Mitford, Gollancz, 1960

How To Dress On £15 A Year As A Lady—By A Lady, published by Frederick Warne & Co, 1873

King Edward VII, Philip Magnus, Murray, 1964

The Language of Field Sports, C. E. Hare, Country Life Ltd, 1949 (revised edition)

Lark Rise To Candleford, Flora Thompson, Oxford University Press, 1945

Life of Benjamin Disraeli, Earl of Beaconsfield, W. F. Monypenny, Murray, 1910.

A Little Book About Great Britain, Azamat Batuk, Bradbury, Evans & Co, 1870

The London Season, Louis T. Stanley, Hutchinson, 1955

London Was Yesterday: 1934–1939, Janet Flanner, Michael Joseph, 1975

Manners and Customs of the English, Percival Leigh, Bradbury & Evans, 1849

Modern Britain, Denis Richards and J. W. Hunt, Longmans, Green & Co, 1950

The Monarchy, L. F. Hobley, Batsford, 1972

Nightrunners of Bengal, John Masters, Michael Joseph, 1951

Notes on England, H. Taine, trans. W. F. Rae, Strahan & Co, 1872 (third English edition)

Ourselves: 1900–1930, Irene Clephane, The Bodley Head, 1933

The Party that Lasted 100 Days, Hilary and Mary Evans, Macdonald and Jane's, 1976

The Perfect Lady, C. Willett Cunnington, Max Parrish, 1948

The Phoenix and the Carpet, E. Nesbit, Benn, 1903

Plain Tales from the Raj, edited by Charles Allen, Andre Deutsch/BBC, 1975

Portraits and Documents: Later Nineteenth Century, 1868–1919, edited by Peter Teed and Michael Clark, Hutchinson Educational, 1969

Pandora's Letter Box: Being A Discourse On Fashionable Life, Doris Langley Moore, Gerald Howe, 1929

Period Piece: A Cambridge Childhood, Gwen Raverat, Faber, 1950

Pleasure of Your Company, June and Doris Langley Moore, Gerald Howe, 1933

Regency People, Ian Grimble, BBC Publications, 1972

Requesting the Pleasure, Ursula Bloom, Robert Hale, 1973

Side-Lights on English Society, E. C. Grenville Murray, Vizetelly & Co, 1881

Sport in England, Norman Wymer, Harrap, 1949

Strawberry Fair: a Biography of Frances, Countess Waldegrave, 1821–79, Osbert Wyndham Hewett, Murray, 1956

The Jeeves Omnibus, P. G. Wodehouse, Herbert Jenkins, 1931

Two Under the Indian Sun, Jon and Rumer Godden, Macmillan, 1966

The Upper Class, Peter Lane, Batsford, 1972

Victorian Cities, Asa Briggs, Odhams, 1963

Victorian Lady Travellers, Dorothy Middleton, Routledge & Kegan Paul, 1965

Victorian New Zealanders, June A. Wood, A. H. & A. W. Reed, 1974

Victorian People in Life and Literature, Gillian Avery, Collins, 1970

Victorian Vista, James Laver, Hulton Press, 1954

The Victorian Woman, Duncan Crow, Allen & Unwin, 1971

Victoria R. I., Elizabeth Longford; Weidenfeld and Nicolson, 1964

Vile Bodies, Evelyn Waugh, Chapman & Hall, 1930

The Woman in Fashion, Doris Langley Moore, Batsford, 1949

Women of the War, Barbara McLaren, Hodder and Stoughton, 1917

The Zoo You Knew?, L. R. Brightwell, Basil Blackwell, 1936

Newspapers and periodicals consulted:

Country Life
Harpers & Queen
Lady
Punch
Sunday Telegraph
The Times

Index